1557

Fa
P484m

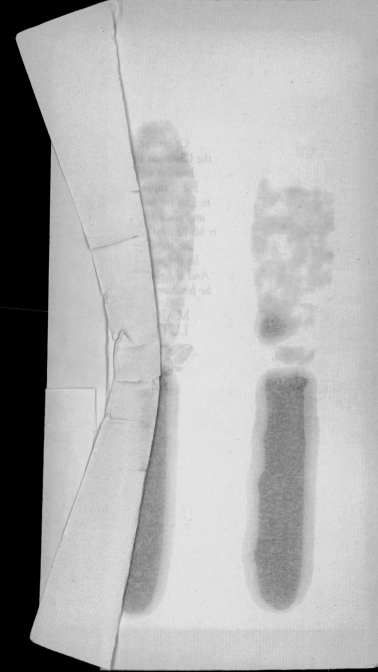

Martin Luther had a Wife

WILLIAM J. PETERSEN

LIVING BOOKS
Tyndale House Publishers, Inc.
Wheaton, Illinois

1557

First printing, February 1983
Library of Congress Catalog Card Number 82-62071
ISBN 0-8423-4104-8, paper
Copyright © 1983 by William J. Petersen
Printed in the United States of America

CONTENTS

INTRODUCTION

MARRIAGES:
Ordinary, Typical, and Others

"Can This Marriage Be Saved?" *Ladies Home Journal* has sold millions of copies on the basis of that long-running magazine series.

Why is it so successful? Because in it you find that other people are encountering the same marital problems (or shall I call them challenges) that you are facing. And often it is easier to get insight into your own problems when you see them in the lives of others.

A look at the marriages of great Christians should provide you with the same kind of insight. At times, as you read these stories you will be asking the same question: "Can this marriage be saved?"

I call these marriages ordinary marriages. By that, I don't mean that they were bad marriages (some were; some weren't) or humdrum marriages (most weren't). I simply mean that they encountered many of the same problems that couples in your church and in your neighborhood are facing.

Nor do I mean that these were typical marriages. Frankly, I'm not sure what a typical marriage is, anyway. I know that some Christian books and magazine articles talk about ideal and idyllic Christian marriages. But as you read about the marriages described in this book, I don't think you'll want to pray, "Lord, I want a carbon copy of that one," because it conforms perfectly to some imaginary ideal.

The reason for that, I suppose, is that there are no typical people. And when you put two atypical people together in a marriage, you don't come up with a typical marriage, whatever that is.

So, to repeat, I think that you will find these to be ordinary marriages, but not typical marriages.

Of course, greatness, like genius, places unusual stress on a marriage. For one thing, leaders are in the spotlight, and nothing grows normally under such conditions. For another thing, the very gifts and character traits that make a person stand out as a leader may make him or her a challenge as a marriage partner. (Notice that this time I didn't say "problem".)

In the case of the evangelists — Wesley and Moody, for example — travel complicated the marriage. How does a wife cope when a husband is away from home so much of the time? You'll discover that John and Molly Wesley were unable to work out a good solution to the problem.

In the case of the unusually gifted wives — consider Catherine Booth for example — you find conventional roles twisted. How did William Booth handle it?

How did Katie Luther manage to live with her bombastic, blustery husband? And how did Sarah Edwards treat a moody, preoccupied genius?

The problems may loom larger because of the magnitude of the characters, but they are the same kinds of problems that you and your friends and neighbors have to handle in a day of working wives, corporate mobility, business travel, and so on.

In this book you will not find extended treatment of the spiritual accomplishments of these men and women. There are many excellent biographies available, and I hope you will be encouraged to read some of them to learn more of how God worked so mightily through these choice servants of His.

But I was more interested in the ingredients of their marriages. So the emphasis here is on their family backgrounds, the courtship, the marriage's early years (always a crucial time of adjustment), the family relationships, and the two personalities involved.

Of course, there are other fascinating marriages in church history — John Calvin, William Carey,

Adoniram Judson, Harriet Beecher Stowe, and Billy Graham, to name but a few, but these five will serve as a sampler to show you that even the greatest Christians of church history have had rather ordinary marriages and have faced the same kinds of problems that each of us face day by day.

It is my prayer that you will learn as many lessons from them as I have.

CHAPTER ONE

Meet Martin and Katie Luther

YOU know about Martin Luther, who sparked the Protestant Reformation by nailing his Ninety-Five Theses to the church door in Wittenberg, Germany. But do you know about his wife, Katie, the runaway nun?

She had a quick tongue and he had a quick temper, a combination that does not usually make for a good marriage.

So what kind of a marriage did Martin and Katie have?

A very *un*usual one.

You'll enjoy Katie's outspokenness as well as Martin's colorful outbursts. Martin and Katie seem so human and so contemporary — almost like next-door neighbors. At first you might wonder how their marriage survived. But the better you get to know them, the better you will understand their secret.

"In domestic affairs I defer to Katie. Otherwise I am led by the Holy Ghost." So said Martin Luther, a bit facetiously, about his wife.

"There's a lot to get used to in the first year of marriage," Luther once admitted. "One wakes up in the morning and finds a pair of pigtails on the pillow which were not there before." For the forty-one-year-old former monk and the twenty-six-year-old former nun, there was a lot more than that to get used to.

"I would not change Katie for France or for Venice," Luther said. Once, however, after Katie had contradicted him in front of dinner guests, he sighed and remarked, "If I should ever marry again, I should hew myself an obedient wife out of stone."

Katie was many things for Martin — a gardener, a cook, a nurse, a cattle-raiser, a bookkeeper, and a brewer. But you could never accuse Katie of being a stone. One biographer calls Katie a "quick-witted Saxon with a ready tongue," which made an interesting match for Luther, an intense debater with a short fuse. She could not be described as beautiful with "her longish head, high forehead, long nose, and powerful chin." It was her intelligence and personality that made her attractive to others.

According to one historian, "She ruled both her household and her husband, a situation which the latter accepted resignedly, since he was totally incapable of organizing the affairs of even the smallest household. She brought order into his life and not always to his satisfaction." Martin would probably change that assessment by saying, "She managed the areas that I delegated to her."

There was nothing romantic about the early days of their marriage; Martin Luther was motivated more by duty than by love in pursuing it, and Katie was marrying on the rebound. Yet undeniably a deep love grew between them. Surprisingly, the marriage of Martin and Katie Luther became a model for Protestant marriage.

Who would have thought a few years earlier that either Martin or Katie would get married? And if, by chance, either one got married, who would have thought that either one would have a happy marriage?

Born November 10, 1483, to a copper miner and his wife in Eisleben on the edge of Germany's Thuringian forest, Martin was raised with the strictness that was characteristic of the day in both home and school. Of his parents' strictness, he later rationalized, "They meant well." Regarding the discipline measures used by his early schoolteachers, he asked, "Whoever loved a schoolmaster anyway?" Later, with his own children, he always made sure that there was an apple alongside the rod.

Throughout life he struggled against overbearing and unreasonable authority. At the same time he wanted to be loved. Sometimes shy, he delighted to be in the spotlight; sometimes crude and earthy, he was also warm and devotionally tender. From his father, he picked up a refreshing sense of humor; from his mother, a love of music. He was often moody, sometimes depressed. An indefatigable worker, he often neglected his own health.

No, Martin Luther was not a simple man.

The first major turning point in his life came when he was twenty-one. He had just received his master's degree from the University of Erfurt, and was on his way to a career in law, as his father had wanted.

He was pleasing his father, but there was a Higher Authority that he seemed incapable of pleasing. He felt the wrath of God dangling precariously over his head. "How can you become pious enough to please a holy God?" he asked himself.

One night as he was returning to law school from his parents' home, he was caught in a violent thunderstorm. A bolt of lightning rent the sky, and the twenty-one-year-old law student begged God to spare him, vowing that he would enter a monastery if He would. And two weeks later, he dismayed his parents and shocked his friends by doing just that.

The vows he took were obedience, poverty, and chastity, which of course ruled out marriage. Withdrawing from the world into the monastery, he devoted himself exclusively to prayer. But he was never satisfied that he had the answer to the question, "How can you become pious enough to please a holy God?"

In a few years he was transferred to a monastery in Wittenberg, and was named lecturer in Bible studies at the new university there. As he began to teach God's Word — particularly the Epistles of Romans and Galatians — he made a new discovery. Righteousness does not come by works; it is imputed to us by faith. It does not come by what we do, but by what Christ has already done in our behalf. He termed it a "wonderful new definition of righteousness." Martin Luther had grasped the meaning of Paul's expression, "The just shall live by faith."

In 1517, when he was thirty-three, Martin Luther nailed his Ninety-Five Theses to the Wittenberg door, seeking a scholarly debate. He never got the debate; he got a Reformation instead.

Four years later, he was called to appear before the Diet of Worms, where Emperor Charles V, Archduke Ferdinand, six Prince Electors, dukes, archbishops, papal nuncios, ambassadors — a total of 200 dignitaries — were gathered. Although he knew his life was at stake, Martin Luther refused to retract what he had written. His authority was not the church nor the Pope; his authority was the Bible itself, the Word of God. "Here I stand. I can do no other. God help me."

A few days later, the Edict of Worms condemned both Luther and his writings and asked all citizens for their help in arresting him. If they preferred, they could kill Luther on sight.

Luther, however, had left Worms before the edict was signed. On the way back to Wittenberg, friends "kidnapped" him and secretly took him to the Castle of Wartburg, where he remained in exile for eight months, translating the Bible into German.

He was thirty-seven years old now, and still considered himself under the vows he had taken when he had entered the monastery sixteen years earlier. Later, he said, "If anyone had told me, when I was at the Diet of Worms: 'In a few years you will have a wife and be sitting at home,' I should not have believed it."

Before Worms, Luther had been a folk hero of all those who were unhappy with the status quo.

While he was in his Wartburg captivity, Luther's reformation started moving in directions that bewildered him. Monks, as well as priests, began to renounce their vows and get married, and this caused Luther to reexamine his own thinking about the vows of celibacy that he had taken.

Luther's first expression was: "Good heavens, they won't give *me* a wife."

Called back to Wittenberg to restore order to the turbulent movement he had spawned, Luther was upset by religious fanatics on one hand and political radicals on the other. Ignorant religionists were led by visions rather than the Word, and in Luther's absence had drawn away some of those that previously had been disciples of the Wittenberg reformer. On the other hand, peasants were rising up against their feudal lords and claiming the backing of Luther's writings.

When Luther disowned their cause, he was no longer their hero. Many even viewed him as a traitor.

In Saxony (east central Germany) Luther was relatively safe because the ruler of Saxony, Frederick the Wise, had promised the reformer protection. But outside of Saxony, he could travel only at his own risk.

Thus in 1525, eight years after he had penned his Ninety-Five Theses in Wittenberg and four years after he had made his courageous "Here I stand" defense at Worms, Luther was hunted by the Pope, hated by the peasants, and harassed by the religious fanatics. At forty-one, he had good reason to feel that the bloom was gone from the Reformation rose.

And that was the year that Martin Luther married. His bride was Katherine von Bora.

Katherine, nearly sixteen years younger than Martin, had been placed in a nunnery when she was only nine or ten years old. Her father had just remarried and Katie's quick wit and sharp tongue did not endear her to her stepmother. So off to the nunnery. Six years later she took her vows.

In the early 1520s, tracts by Martin Luther began appearing mysteriously within the cloistered walls of Katie's nunnery. Furthermore, rumors had been circulating that elsewhere nuns and monks were leaving their monastic houses to follow this man who was teaching that salvation was a gift from God, not to be earned by religious observances.

Secretly Katie and eleven other nuns sent word to Luther in Wittenberg that they were interested in leaving the nunnery. Could he help them? Security, however, was tight and the nunnery was located in territory ruled by Duke George, an archenemy of Luther. Already Duke George had executed one man for devising an escape plan for some nuns. Luther had to come up with a foolproof plan.

In the nearby town of Torgau was a respected senior citizen named Leonard Kopp. A member of the town council and a former Torgau tax collector, he had the contract to deliver barrels of smoked herring to the cloister in Nimbschen which housed the twelve unhappy nuns. Exactly how Kopp did it is unknown, but somehow when he arrived, his canvas-covered wagon seemed to be carrying twelve barrels of smoked herring, and when he left it seemed to be loaded with twelve empty barrels underneath the canvas. But the barrels were not empty.

Two days later, nine nuns (three had returned to their parents' homes) were delivered to Martin Luther's doorstep, and it was Luther's job to find either positions or husbands for them. Finding jobs for them wouldn't be easy. The nuns weren't trained in housekeeping. One historian commented, "All they could do was pray and sing." To find husbands for them would not be easy either. Since German girls usually married at age fifteen or sixteen, most of the nuns were considerably past their prime. But Martin Luther felt obligated to help them. "I feel so sorry for them; they are a wretched little bunch," he wrote to a friend.

Someone suggested that maybe Luther could help solve his problem by marrying one of them himself. He responded that he wouldn't think of it, not because he was a sexless stone or against marriage, but because he thought he might soon be killed as a heretic. Evidently by this time, he no longer considered himself obligated to continue his monk's vow.

Eventually, Luther was able to find husbands for some of the nuns, but one of them remained as his biggest problem. It was Katie von Bora, who had found temporary employment in the home of Lucas Cranach, Luther's neighbor. Cranach had a large household and he seemed to need all the domestic help he could get.

It wasn't as if no one wanted her. Her personality and quick wit attracted the attention of a young man from a distinguished family in Nuremburg, and the two fell in love. But when he returned to tell his parents that he wished to marry a runaway nun, they refused him permission.

The rejection struck Katie hard, and she was heartbroken. But Luther the matchmaker didn't give up trying. Determined to find a husband for Katie, he soon had someone else in mind. Unfortunately the next candidate didn't suit Katie, though Luther thought that she could ill afford to be fussy. Katie sent word back that while she wasn't at all against the idea of marriage, she would never marry the latest candidate; in fact, to underscore her willingness to marry, she thought she would mention a couple possible candidates herself — even though it was obvious to friends that she was still in love with the young man from Nuremburg. Amsdorf, one of Luther's fellow professors at Wittenberg, was one candidate that she would be willing to marry; the other was Luther himself. Amsdorf, like Luther, was in his early forties.

The message from Katie got back to Luther at a very propitious time. Rumors had been circulating across Europe of the nine nuns who had been camping on Luther's doorstep. Luther's enemies — and they were legion — imagined the worst. There were jokes about Luther's harem. Katie was the only one left, and the rumors were stronger than ever. There was only one nun, but now there were nine times as many rumors.

In April 1525, shortly after he received Katie's message about the two eligible candidates for her hand, Martin visited his aged parents. His father, who had never wanted his son to become a monk, was pleased that Martin had left the monastery. Now only one thing remained before his son could say that he had made a complete break with the past. He would have to marry and father children to carry on the family name.

Luther had been preaching for several years that marriage was a divinely established institution. To elevate celibacy above marriage was unbiblical. Now it was time for him to practice what he had been preaching.

It was a big step for the forty-one-year-old monk to take. With the exception of his parents, he seemed to take counsel with no one else. Even many of his closest friends were unaware of the decision he was struggling with.

Some of his friends had deserted him. His national popularity had waned and his spiritual impact was fragmenting. In some ways, he felt he would have to start all over again. Perhaps at age forty-one he could begin afresh.

What better way than to get married and start a family? As he thought about it, his marriage would "please his father, rile the Pope, make angels laugh and devils weep, and would seal his testimony." Perhaps it would even shut the mouths of the rumormongers.

And hadn't Katie practically proposed to him?

The closest thing to a counter-proposal came when he told Katie that he might be burned at the stake, and if she was wed to him, it might mean her life as well. Apparently, the peril didn't dissuade Katie.

The courtship was anything but romantic. "I am not madly in love, but I cherish her," said Luther.

On June 10, 1525, Luther wrote, "The gifts of God must be taken on the wing." So once he made up his mind, Luther didn't waste any time.

The wedding took place June 13. Lucas Cranach and his wife were witnesses. The suddenness of it caused more rumors to fly and even some close friends like Philipp Melanchthon had second thoughts about it. But as Luther later remarked, "If I had not married quickly and secretly and taken few into my confidence, everyone would have done what he could to hinder me; for all my friends said: 'Not this one, but another.' " Many of them thought that Luther should have married a more distinguished woman than Katie, the runaway nun.

Even Luther had to pinch himself to make sure it wasn't a dream. "I can hardly believe it myself," he joked, "but the witnesses are too strong." And when he invited the herring distributor Leonard Kopp to the wedding, he wrote, "God likes to work miracles and to make a fool of the world. You must come to the wedding."

Their first recorded argument came over a wedding gift — a present of twenty guilders (about two months' salary for Martin) given by Archbishop Albrecht of Mainz. Albrecht was an enemy and Luther wanted nothing to do with his guilders. After all, it was Albrecht who had authorized the selling of indulgences which had prompted Luther's Ninety-Five Theses.

But thrifty Katie, who had picked up some household economics from her experience in the Cranach home, knew that Martin had an indebtedness of one hundred guilders, and she felt that a wedding gift of twenty guilders should be received as from the Lord, no matter through whose hands it may have passed. Luther gave in. The practical outweighed the emotional.

For both of them, the first year of marriage meant great adjustments. Martin had not made his bed in a year. "Before I married, no one had made up my bed for a whole year. The straw was rotting from my sweat. I wore myself out with work during the day, so that I fell into bed oblivious of everything." That was changed now. Katie even gave him a pillow.

For someone who had lived alone as long as Martin had, it wasn't easy to take someone else's views into consideration, but Katie's personality injected itself forcefully into Martin's decision-making processes. For instance, he had planned to go to a friend's wedding. When he told Katie where it was, she put up a fuss. Marauding bands of peasants were known to be in the area and they were angry about some of Luther's writings. Katie thought it would be unwise to travel through their territory. Luther deferred to Katie's judgment.

But Martin's biggest adjustment dealt with the family's purse strings. He had never learned how to handle money. He once said, "God divided the hand into fingers so that money would slip through." He was "loath to accept anything not absolutely necessary, and he would give away anything not absolutely required."

With Katie as his business manager, fiscal planning was introduced. As one biographer puts it, Frau Luther's thrift enabled the Luthers to "accumulate a considerable property, notwithstanding her husband's unbounded liberality and hospitality." At times she had to hide money to keep Martin from giving it away. Martin would invite students to come and live with them, but Katie insisted that they pay room and board.

The Wittenberg bank didn't appreciate Martin's penchant for overdrawing his account, but he explained with a strange lack of logic, "I do not worry about debts anymore, because when Katie pays one, another comes due."

While there were tensions in this area, Martin soon came to understand his deficiencies and Katie's strengths in household management. "The greatest blessing," Luther once wrote, probably thinking of Katie, "is to have a wife to whom you may entrust your affairs."

There is some indication that early in his marriage Martin was concerned enough about their financial situation to do something about it. He installed a lathe, perhaps thinking that he could go into business if his government stipend was cut off. There is no record that he ever used the lathe, however, and his philosophy was always "The Lord will provide."

Martin's best work was done in front of books, not in front of a lathe.

He had to adjust to working with people around him. In the monastery he had been accustomed to being secluded, but Katie wouldn't stand for that. According to one story, he once locked himself in his study for three days until Katie had the door removed. Innocently, Martin asked as he saw Katie standing in the doorless doorway, "Why did you do that? I wasn't doing any harm."

Katie wasn't content to be a Martha, working in the kitchen or garden. But Luther didn't always want to be bothered by a Mary. She liked to sit at Martin's side while he read. "During the first year," Martin told some friends, "my Katie would sit at my side while I was working, and when she was at a loss for something to say, she would ask me: 'Is the Grand Master of Prussia the brother of the Margrave?' "

Even after the children came — and they had six children — Martin, who was adjusting well to doing his work in a fishbowl atmosphere, often wanted to withdraw into himself at the time when Katie wanted to share his world. As biographer Roland Bainton points out, "The rhythm of work and rest did not coincide for Luther and his wife. After a day with children, animals and servants, she wanted to talk with an equal; and he, after preaching four times, lecturing and conversing with students at meals, wanted to drop into a chair and sink into a book." And then Katie might ask him a question about the Grand Master of Prussia or about predestination or why David in the Psalms bragged about his own righteousness when he really didn't have any.

"All my life is patience," said Luther, who must have recognized that patience wasn't his strongest virtue. "I have to be patient with the Pope; I have to be patient with the heretics; I have to be patient with my family; and I even have to be patient with Katie." Katie had to be even more patient with her genius husband. He was a man of many moods; melancholy was often induced by poor health, and sometimes vice versa. "I think that my illnesses are not natural, but are mere bewitchments," he once said. Another time, he said, "I am so ill, but no one believes me." He had a shopping list of ailments including gout, insomnia, catarrh, hemorrhoids, constipation, stone (gallstones or kidney stones), dizziness, and ringing in the ears.

Katie patiently nursed him back to health with proper diet, herbs, poultices, and massages. But once after she gave him some medicine for his migraine headaches, he responded: "My best prescription is written in the third chapter of John: 'For God so loved the world, that he gave his only begotten Son, that whosoever believeth in him should not perish, but have eternal life.' "

Katie was far more than chief cook, nurse, and bottle-washer. She had to be a remarkable woman to manage the ever-expanding Luther household. The Augustinian monastery where Luther had lived as a monk was deeded to Martin and Katie jointly by the government. On the first floor it had forty rooms with cells above for sleeping; at times every room was occupied. Besides the six Luther children, a half dozen of Martin's nieces and nephews were brought in, out of the goodness of his heart. Then when a friend lost his wife in a plague, Luther brought home the four children. To cope with the growing household, Katie in turn brought in some of her relatives, including Aunt Magdalena, who became a "nanny" for the Luther children and was nicknamed Mummie Lena.

Besides the children, there were tutors and student boarders, and of course due to Luther's fame, guests dropped in unexpectedly from England, Hungary, and elsewhere. One prince had been planning to take a room at the monastery for a few days, but changed his mind. He had received a letter, telling him the nature of the place: "An odd assortment of young people, students, young widows, old women and children lives in the Doctor's home; this makes for great disquiet."

But more and more the gregarious Luther thrived in the bustling atmosphere. The students who got the benefit of Luther's formal lectures during the day plied him with questions during the supper hour and the reformer's famed *Table Talks* emerged. Katie would be at the far end of the table surrounded by the children while the students were taking notes close to her husband. No doubt, she was a bit jealous that they were able to get closer to Dr. Luther than she could at the supper hour, but she knew her husband needed the attention. When she found out that the students were taking notes which they intended to publish, however, she wanted to charge them for note-taking privileges. Martin wouldn't let her do it. Later these students published 6596 entries in their various versions of *Table Talks*. If Katie had had her way, she would have had a guilder for each entry.

At times, during these informal supper sessions, Luther's language became coarse or crude and Katie would have to rebuff him: "Oh, come now, that's too raw."

That happened often enough, for Luther was not known for delicacy of speech. But more often than that, he would spend the entire supper hour talking. When Katie, who didn't mince words, would say, "Doctor, why don't you stop talking and eat?" he would respond with something like: "Women should repeat the Lord's Prayer before opening their mouths."

Katie called him "Doctor" in public conversation. Martin called her anything that came into his mind. Sometimes thinking of Eve, he called her "my rib." More often, thinking of the way she managed the manor, he called her "my lord." Sometimes, he called her "my chain," a pun on the German *Kethe*.

During the day, children played in Martin Luther's study. Once he told of his son Hans: "As I sit and write, he sings me a song, and if it gets too loud I scold him a little, but he goes on singing just the same."

Luther says he learned much from his children, although he was amused by their silly play: "Christ said we must become as little children to enter the kingdom of heaven. Dear God, this is too much. Have we got to become such idiots?"

Besides being a good mother and efficient housekeeper, Katie proved to be a wise manager of the farms, gardens, cattle, and livestock that the Luther family came to own, thanks to her prudent and expansive policies. She also took care of the small family brewery, and Luther frequently praised his wife's ability to make good beer.

Katie remodelled the monastery, installing a bathroom and putting in three cellars with an extra stairway. Because she had a goal to make their large household self-supporting, she grew peas, beans, turnips, melons, and lettuce in their vegetable garden and eight different fruits in their orchard. (One year, her husband magnanimously took care of the garden.) Begrudgingly, Martin gave his consent to her to buy a second garden. The deciding factor was that a brook ran through it. Katie was able to hook quite a few fish from the brook for their supper table. Their livestock included eight pigs, five cows, nine calves, as well as chickens, pigeons, geese, and a dog named Tolpel that Luther hoped to meet in heaven. All of these were Katie's responsibility, and she even played the role of veterinary surgeon to do the job properly.

Martin wasn't exactly happy about the fact that Katie inherited a farm in Zulsdorf, a two-day journey from Wittenberg. He didn't appreciate the amount of time that Katie spent there; for Katie it was a retreat from the hubbub of the Wittenberg monastery.

One letter Martin wrote her was addressed: "To the rich lady of Zulsdorf, who lives in the flesh at Wittenberg, but in the spirit at Zulsdorf."

Her land was her empire, and like an emperor she always had her mind set on conquering new worlds and annexing them to her kingdom. One farm she looked at was only an hour away from Wittenberg. Martin stalled her long enough to give someone else the time to buy it. Once Martin wrote her, "Oh, Katie, you have a husband who loves you. Let someone else be an empress."

In a letter to a friend, Martin once wrote: "My lord Katie greets you. She plants our fields, pastures and sells cows et cetera. In between she has started to read the Bible. I have promised her fifty guilders if she finishes by Easter. She is hard at it and is at the end of the fifth book of Moses."

It's a wonder that she had time to read the book of Jude, much less the entire Bible. But Luther kept on prodding her to keep at her Bible reading, until she responded, "Would to God I lived up to it!"

When Katie became frustrated with a project, she was apt to strike her side and burst forth with an "Ave Maria," to which Luther would respond, "Why don't you ask Christ to help you?"

They teased each other in good humor. Once while he was traveling, Luther wrote home: "To the saintly, worrying Lady Katherine Luther, doctor at Zulsdorf [the home of her inherited farm] and Wittenberg, my gracious, dear wife. We thank you heartily for being so worried that you can't sleep, for since you started worrying about us, a fire broke out near my door, and yesterday, no doubt due to your worry, a big stone, save for the dear angels, would have fallen and crushed us like a mouse in a trap. If you don't stop worrying, I'm afraid the earth will swallow us. Pray and let God worry. Cast your burden on the Lord."

Martin's appreciation of marriage deepened during his twenty years with Katie. Marriage is a school for character, and both he and Katie learned much in that school. They learned from each other, from their children, and from their mutual experiences. The father, said Luther one day, even learns from his experience of hanging out the diapers to the amusement of his neighbors. "Let them laugh," he concluded. "God and the angels smile in heaven."

He thought of the miracle at Cana in John 2 as a parable of marriage. "The first love," he once said, "is drunken. When the intoxication wears off, then comes the real married love." The best wine is saved for last. There may be times when it may appear that the wine is running out. "I will not take the vexation out of marriage. I may even increase it, but it will turn out wonderfully, as they only know who have tasted it."

Since both Martin and Katie had quick tongues, arguments were not foreign to the Luther household. "But," said Martin, "think of all the squabbles Adam and Eve must have had in the course of their 900 years. Eve would say, 'You ate the apple' and Adam would retort, 'You gave it to me.' "

With all the bantering, the Luthers had a good marriage. "To have peace and love in marriage is a gift which is next to the knowledge of the Gospel," he once said. And no one could deny that the Luthers had that gift.

Before his marriage, Luther sometimes spoke of matrimony as a necessity for the flesh. Afterwards, he emphasized it was an opportunity for the spirit. He came to decry the fact that many men were marrying only for physical reasons, were abusing their wives, and knew nothing about love. Marriage is no joke, he said; it must be worked on, and prayed over. . . . "To get a wife is easy enough, but to love her with constancy is difficult...for the mere union of the flesh is not sufficient; there must be a congeniality of tastes and character. And that congeniality does not come overnight.

"Some marriages were motivated by mere lust," Luther once said, "but mere lust is felt even by fleas and lice. Love begins when we wish to serve others.

"Of course, the Christian should love his wife," Luther declared. "He is supposed to love his neighbor, and since his wife is his nearest neighbor, she should be his deepest love. And she should also be his dearest friend."

That this friendship existed between Martin and Katie is obvious from the frequency of Luther's references to his wife. When he spoke of Paul's Epistle to the Galatians, the reading of which led to his spiritual rebirth, he called it "my Katharina von Bora." It was the epistle that was the closest to his heart.

Once when he was stressing the importance of trusting Christ in daily matters, he confessed: "I trust more in Katie and I expect more from Katie than I do Christ." Perhaps it testified more to his relationship with his wife than it did to a lack of commitment to Jesus Christ.

"Nothing is more sweet than harmony in marriage, and nothing more distressing than dissension," Luther said and no doubt his marriage had moments of both. "Next to it is the loss of a child. I know how that hurts."

The Luthers lost their second child before she was a year old and their third, Magdalena, in her fourteenth year. "How strange it is that she is at peace and I am so sorrowful," he said at her death.

But children brought much joy to the home. Referring to his children, he said, "God has given to me greater gifts than to any bishop in a thousand years." Yet the children were certainly normal, active youngsters. To one of them, Luther cried out, "Child, what have you done that I should love you so? What with your befouling the corners and bawling through the whole house." In 1531, watching Katie fondle their youngest son, Martin, he remarked, "Surely God must talk with me even more fondly than my Katie with her little Martin."

When Luther was fifty-nine, their daughter Magdalena died. It was a severe blow to Luther at a time when he was beset with other trials as well.

His health was worsening and he was involved in several major religious disputes.

Outside the home, he was becoming increasingly bitter, cantankerous, and unbending. Some of his friends felt that he might undo all that he had accomplished in his earlier years. But the home was a refuge for him and there is no indication that Luther's external problems soured its atmosphere.

On his deathbed, Luther admonished: "If it be God's will, accept it." Katie responded: "My dear doctor, if it is God's will, I would rather have you with our Lord than here. Don't worry about us. God will take care of us."

In 1546 at the age of sixty-two, Martin died. Katie died four years later. Her last words were "I will stick to Christ as a burr to a topcoat."

Martin may have been the key figure in the Protestant Reformation, but Martin and Katie together revolutionized the common concept of marriage that was held in that day.

There was a saying that Martin loved to quote: "Let the wife make her husband glad to come home and let him make her sorry to see him leave."

The success of any marriage depends on two people who aren't afraid to grow and change as Martin and Katie did.

CHAPTER TWO

Meet John and Molly Wesley

MOST of you don't need to be introduced to John Wesley, the father of the worldwide Methodist movement. You sing the hymns written by John and his brother Charles. You are aware of his Aldersgate experience, and the entire world has been affected by John's concerns for evangelism and personal holiness.

But you have probably never encountered Molly Goldhawk Vazeille Wesley, John's wife.

Maybe, after I've introduced you, you will wish you had never met her.

I can guarantee, however, as you interact with John and Molly, that you will have much cause for thought.

What were the factors that made it such a miserable marriage?

How could it have been otherwise?

What can you learn from it to avoid in your own marriage?

One of the early Wesley biographers stated that, along with Xanthippe and Job's wife, Mrs. John Wesley had to be rated as one of the worst wives in all history.

A later biographer responded by saying that if that was so, then surely John Wesley must be regarded as one of the worst husbands in history.

Both allegations seem quite extreme.

But what are you to do with the story that Molly Wesley was seen dragging her husband around the room by his hair?

And what about the correspondence that John Wesley continued to maintain, despite his wife's objections, with his female admirers?

John Wesley is well known as the intrepid evangelist of Methodism who traveled a quarter of a million miles on horseback, who claimed the world as his parish, and who rose at four each morning for his devotional time. But his home was a shambles. Four years after his marriage, he wrote to his brother Charles, "Love is rot."

He preached 42,000 sermons, often preaching four or five times a day during his fifty-three-year ministry. Crowds of up to 30,000 came to hear him preach. When he died at the age of eighty-eight, Methodism had 153,000 adherents, and the movement had spread to America as well as to Holland, Ireland, and Scotland.

He was a remarkable man and God used him mightily. Yet his marriage was a miserable failure.

He waited for marriage until he was forty-seven; he probably waited too long. (Some would say he didn't wait long enough.) He had serious romances when he was twenty-five, thirty-five, and forty-five. He retreated from each one at the last minute. Perhaps any one of the three would have provided him a happier marriage than he had with Molly. But had Wesley had a happier marriage, we might not have had the outgrowth of the formidable Methodist movement.

In order to understand John Wesley and his problems in marriage, you have to take a glimpse of the fascinating home in which he was reared.

John Wesley was the fifteenth of nineteen children born to Samuel and Susanna Wesley. Samuel was a stern, argumentative Anglican cleric who spent most of his ministry in an out-of-the-way parish, trying to exhort a bunch of uneducated ruffians. His biggest joy in life seemed to be when he could get away from Epworth to go to Convocation in London. It had been an honor for him to be named to this top-ranking study commission; it was a joy as well because during the sessions he got to argue theology with eminent theologians.

At home, he argued with his wife, Susanna, a well-educated, well-bred woman who wanted the best for her husband and for her children, and who had a reason for everything she did.

Both Susanna and Samuel were stubborn, and Samuel had a quick temper besides. Once during family prayers, after Samuel had properly prayed for the reigning English monarch, King William of Orange, he noted that his wife had not said her traditional "amen." In fact, come to think of it, she had not said the appropriate "amen" for several days. The reason was obvious. Susanna did not favor King William of Orange; she thought he was a usurper of the throne. She favored the Stuart line. So, in Susanna's words, her husband "immediately kneeled down and imprecated the divine vengeance upon himself and all his posterity if ever he touched me more or came into bed with me before I had begged God's pardon and his."

Whereupon Samuel left for a timely Convocation in London. King William soon died, which was an answer to prayer for Susanna and maybe even for the equally stubborn Samuel, because upon William's death Queen Anne, a Stuart, came to the throne. Thereafter Susanna could say "amen" when her husband prayed for the reigning monarch.

The story is typical of the marriage. Here are some quotes from Susanna's writings: "Since I'm willing to let him quietly enjoy his opinions, he ought not to deprive me of my little liberty of conscience." And "I think we are not likely to live happily together." And another, "It is a misfortune peculiar to our family that he and I seldom think alike."

A little more than nine months after the coronation of Queen Anne, John Wesley, the fifteenth of the Wesleys' nineteen children, was born. Nine of the children died at birth or in infancy, and that left ten to be raised on the modest income derived from the remote parish of Epworth. When John — or "Jackie" as his mother called him — was only two years old, his father was imprisoned for three months for his inability to pay a thirty-pound debt. During his prison term, his biggest concern was his family, but he wrote, "My wife bears it with the courage which becomes her and which I expected from her."

Later when Samuel was in London attending another of the lengthy Convocations, an interim minister preached in his pulpit and made repeated aspersions about the regular minister's chronic indebtedness and about other foibles that Samuel undeniably had.

When the congregation dwindled, Susanna began holding evening services in her kitchen. Soon her evening flock outnumbered those in the morning congregation at the Epworth church. The interim rector didn't like it. He wrote to Samuel in London urging him to take immediate action and stop this outrage. Simultaneously, Susanna wrote, justifying her actions. Something needed to be done, she said, and no man in the congregation had as strong a voice as she had; furthermore no one else could read well enough to lead the congregation in the prayerbook and the reading of the sermon. She said that although she knew that God approved of what she was doing, she would submit to her husband if he would definitely put his foot down. But he had to say so definitely. Then she asked her husband if he wanted to put his foot down or not. The way she wrote it was like this: "Do not tell me that you desire me not to do it, for that will not satisfy my conscience; but send me your positive command in such full and express terms as may absolve me from all guilt and punishment for neglecting this opportunity of doing good, when you and I shall appear before the great and awful tribunal of our Lord Jesus Christ."

Samuel Wesley decided that since the problem would go away as soon as he returned home in a few weeks, he would take no immediate action.

As if the Wesleys didn't have enough troubles, the old parsonage caught fire one night in 1709. Nearly everything was lost, but fortunately the children had all escaped to the garden. All except one. Five-year-old John was missing. The father tried to reenter the house but the smoke and flames made the stairway impassable. Finally a ladder was brought and was raised to little John's window. The boy was saved, just before the roof collapsed.

Susanna called it divine intervention and spoke of John as "a brand plucked from the burning." After the dramatic rescue, while she was mindful of the spiritual welfare of all her children, she was especially concerned about young John. She had made a resolution to be "particularly careful of the soul of this child, which God had so mercifully provided for."

Susanna raised her children strictly. At the age of one year, they were instructed to cry softly when they had to cry. She took responsibility for their early education, and her daughters were treated as the educational equals of her sons. She regimented her spiritual activities and expected her children to do accordingly. She assigned a day of the week when she would take time to provide personalized scriptural and moral instruction to her children. Each child was assigned a day; John's day was Thursday.

Growing up, John was tended by seven sisters. Later most of the sisters, like John himself, experienced unhappy marriages. Where the blame lies for the string of mismatches is hard to tell. Some blame the father who had a knack for crushing his daughters' promising love affairs, until in rebellion they ran off with totally unsuitable mates. One of the daughters openly spoke of the father's "unaccountable love of discord." His paternal concern made him censorious and overly protective.

Samuel Wesley was a man who had never come to terms with himself. His parish was too small and remote. He wasn't properly appreciated in the community. At home he was frustrated by his inability to cope with Susanna and his children. And at times this frustration erupted irrationally.

Susanna herself was such a dominant force that her influence was indelibly imprinted on her children's personalities — especially on John's. She was John's spiritual advisor until her death when John was thirty-nine. For years they read and discussed the same books. One biographer says: "Hers was the decisive voice that sent her two sons on their ill-starred mission to Georgia; it was to her steadfastness that John looked for reassurance when he returned to England with his faith shaken and his future in jeopardy. As soon as he had a settled home, his mother became its permanent inmate. He himself admitted that in his early youth he put aside all thoughts of marriage through despair of finding any woman her equal."

John Wesley grew up with his mother's logical mind. His brother Charles was heir to their father's poetic flair. But John became a skilled debater with a love for wit and humor. His wit and humor made him quite popular during his youth. One of his sisters said that no one could be sad when John was around.

At seventeen, John went to Oxford University where he studied the classics and had his first serious romance. One of the earliest entries in his diary, which he kept for more than sixty years, asks, "Have I loved a woman or company more than God?" It was a question that plagued him through the years.

There were four young women in a circle of friends, and John had an interest in each of them. He wrote to his mother about Betty Kirkham, describing her as a "religious friend," but it is obvious from his diary that she was a special kind of religious friend. However, after waiting several years for John's expressions of affection to materialize in a proposal of marriage, Betty Kirkham accepted the hand of another suitor. His diary indicates that he had thought of marriage, but something had kept him from it.

He kept his friendship with Betty alive for several years — even though her husband was jealous of Wesley's attention to his wife. John at the same time was beginning his solicitations of another young woman in the circle. When the only way the relationship could progress any further was by a proposal of marriage, John backed away again.

Mabel Brailsford in her *Tale of Two Brothers* writes: "The pattern had now been set for all John's abortive love affairs: the bright beginning, the hesitation and long shilly-shallying: the exasperation of the lady and her ultimatum, quickly rescinded but not quickly enough to forestall his final renunciation. Three times he would be upon the brink of marriage and three times he would extricate himself before the decisive word had been spoken. Each time his affections were more deeply involved."

John was twenty-nine now, had his master's degree from Oxford, had been appointed a teaching fellow and had, with his brother Charles, started the "Holy Club," a group that because of its methodical way of attaining spirituality became known as the Methodists.

His seventy-year-old father wanted him to take over his parish at Epworth, but John refused the offer, wanting to stay at Oxford, where he could promote his own holiness. He told his father that only where he himself could be holy could he effectively promote the holiness of others.

At this point in his life, John preferred the role of tutor to that of professor. He wanted to disciple those who were earnestly seeking the path of salvation. But he had two problems: (1) he was not sure of his own salvation and (2) he was very naive about those who pretended to be spiritually minded, especially young spiritually minded women. To be blunt, John was much more attractive to women than he realized.

This was clearly seen in 1735 when he was appointed as a chaplain to accompany James Oglethorpe to the new colony of Georgia in America. John's job in America would be to assist the motley band of settlers — ex-convicts, Jews, German exiles, and debtors — and to preach to the heathen Indians whom he considered to be "little children, humble, willing to learn." But Wesley's main reason for going to America was simply in his own words: "My chief motive, to which all the rest are subordinate, is the hope of saving my own soul." He was also quite certain that in Georgia he would no longer be tempted by the lusts of the flesh for he would "no longer see any woman, but those which are almost of a different species from me."

He didn't realize how wrong he was.

On board ship, John was "in jeopardy every hour," as he wrote in his diary. He thought of asking his brother Charles to pray for him, because of the many young women aboard, some of whom were feigning spiritual interest. He felt he needed prayer that he should "know none of them after the flesh."

When a storm arose on the Atlantic, he realized he was in jeopardy another way. The German Moravians on board seemed to be the only passengers who were calm in the face of what seemed to John to be a possible grave in the angry deep. When John asked the reason for their serenity, he in return was asked a few questions: "Do you know Jesus Christ?" "Do you know you are a child of God?" "Do you know you are saved?"

John was perplexed. He was a minister and a son of a minister. He was even a missionary and he was rigorously practicing holiness, elusive though it was, and he was intent on pursuing it even if his chase took him around the world. But he had to admit that he did not possess the calm assurance of salvation that the Moravians had.

After arriving on *terra firma* in America, things did not improve. Though he attended to his disciplines faithfully — arising at four, services at five, etc. — he was ineffective both as a minister to the settlers and as a missionary to the Indians.

But he was not ineffective in reaching the heart of Sophy Hopkey, the eighteen-year-old niece of Savannah's chief magistrate. John, now thirty-three, found in Sophy everything he wanted in a woman. She was "all stillness and attention" when he read books of sermons to her. She was quick to learn when he instructed her in French grammar. She was also quite ready for marriage, since she was unhappy at home with her aunt and uncle.

John didn't know what to do. When he was with her, he confessed that he was under the weight of "an unholy desire." He admitted to her that he would like to spend the rest of his life with her. Half the colony, it seemed, was urging him to marry the girl, but John pulled away from the flame. "I find, Miss Sophy, I cannot take fire into my bosom and not be burnt. I am therefore retiring for awhile to desire the direction of God."

Getting away from Sophy didn't solve the problem. So for his definitive answer on whether to get married or not, he decided to draw lots. One slip of paper said, "Marry"; another, "Not this year"; a third, "Think of it no more." The third slip of paper was drawn.

Though John still found it difficult, he broke up with Sophy. By the end of the year, John had returned to England. In his journal, he described his break with Sophy as an escape, and that once again he was "a brand snatched from the burning." On his way back to England, he had several weeks to think about his missionary term in America. It had lasted less than two years, and John was realistic enough to assess it as a failure.

But six months later, Wesley's new life began. Depressed, he attended a meeting near Aldersgate Street in London and listened to the reading of Luther's *Commentary on Romans*. Wesley felt his heart "strangely warmed." He had been converted. He had discovered "salvation by faith only." Now he knew Jesus as the German Moravians did.

A year later, in 1739, Wesley began his preaching in the fields. The crowds were huge. Wesley estimated twenty thousand at some of the preaching services. Quickly the work expanded. A school for poor children was started at Kingswood; a new meeting house was built in Bristol. An old cannon foundry near Moorfields was transformed into a 1500-seat chapel.

During the next fifty years, he crisscrossed England on horseback over rough country roads, preaching the gospel nine months a year, starting

Methodist societies all across the British Isles. Wesley became one of the dominant figures of the eighteenth century.

It was during the early years of this itinerant ministry that he met Grace Murray and entered into his most serious love affair. Grace Murray was in her late twenties, the widow of a sailor. Converted by Wesley's preaching, she soon became the leading woman Methodist, addressing the women's classes.

In 1748, Wesley, now forty-five, became ill and was tended by the "amiable, pious and efficient" Mrs. Murray. John didn't exactly propose to her on the spot, but he did say, "If ever I marry, I think you will be the person." The widow Murray was flattered by his attention.

When Wesley was well enough to resume his preaching schedule, Grace was asked to join the troupe. A few months later John conducted evangelistic missions in Ireland and Grace was once again a part of his team. In fact, she rode on the same horse behind Wesley. Wesley reported on her ministry, "She examined all the women in the smaller societies, and the believers in every place. She settled all the women bands, visited the sick, prayed with the mourners." She was, as one report has stated, the only coworker with whom John was able to work closely for a long period of time.

John was deeply in love with Grace and he debated the pros and cons of matrimony. As usual, he kept a scorecard. In all seven marriage areas (housekeeper, nurse, companion, friend, fellow-laborer in the gospel of Christ, spiritual gifts, and spiritual fruit from her labors), he rated Grace as excellent. He concluded, "Therefore all my seven arguments against marriage are totally set aside. Nay some of them seem to prove, both that I ought to marry and that G. M. is the Person." G. M. was his business-efficient way of referring to Grace Murray.

John realized that there might be some problems. For instance, what about children? His solution would be to place the children in the Methodist school at Kingswood while he and his wife continued their evangelistic ministry. One writer commented: "He was incapable of real domesticity; he wanted a coadjutor, not a wife."

But John faced some other obstacles too, the biggest of which was his own procrastination. And then there was the promise that he had made to the Holy Club not to marry without their permission. That meant that he needed to get the approval of his brother Charles, among others.

Grace was not happy with John's dillydallying. One of John's helpers, John Bennett, was waiting in the wings for Grace, and he was ready to step in whenever John Wesley's ardor cooled. Prior to Wesley's coming on the scene, it was Bennett who had been Grace Murray's suitor. During a lull in the action, Wesley had entered, center-stage. Bennett was still available.

Some Methodist leaders thought it wouldn't

look right for Wesley to marry Grace Murray. It would look as if she had been his mistress during the past several years of evangelistic forays. Others felt for John to marry someone not of his social class would be a horrible mistake. They thought it would split the movement.

That's when his brother Charles Wesley stepped in. "Jumped in" would be a more accurate phrase. In his opinion, the entire Methodist movement would go down the drain if John married. Any other minister in the movement could marry, but John was a special case. Besides, if John married Grace, Charles thought that half of the leadership would pack their bags. John's diary records his brother's feelings this way: "The thought of marrying at all, but especially of my marrying a servant and one so low-born, appeared above measure shocking to him."

Charles didn't have a moment to spare. Hurriedly, he jumped on his horse and galloped to see Grace. He convinced her that if she went ahead with marriage to John, it "would destroy himself and the whole work of God." Two hours later, he took Grace away, brought her to Bennett, convinced both of them that for the good of Methodism they should marry each other, and in a few days the marriage took place.

John was irate — understandably so. His brother's chicanery was inexcusable. The lifelong close relationship between John and Charles was nearly severed. Gradually, forgiveness came, but not much more. "I can forgive, but who can redress the wrong?" John wrote. Soon, however, John was back on his horse, riding his evangelistic circuit again with the words: "The Lord gave, and the Lord hath taken away; blessed be the name of the Lord."

One biographer doubts that Wesley would ever have married Grace Murray, despite what he had told her: "There can be no doubt that John Wesley delighted to dream of Grace Murray as his promised wife, but in view of his past history, the question arises whether even without Charles' intervention, that promise would ever have become performance."

But fifteen months later, John Wesley did get married, and he was determined that no one would ride off with his bride this time.

One of the few Methodist stalwarts who took John Wesley's side in his disagreement with his brother was Vincent Perronet. Perronet felt that John needed to be married; in fact, he urged it upon him as a duty. At this point, John probably didn't need much urging. Perronet consulted with Banker Ebenezer Blackwell and came up with a candidate, Molly Vazeille, the widow of a London merchant who had left her an inheritance of ten thousand pounds.

With Grace, John Wesley had a checklist to see if his bride-to-be measured up. With Molly, there was no checklist. With Grace, John consulted his brother in advance, and that proved to be a mistake. With Molly, John didn't consult his brother, and that also proved to be a mistake.

He didn't consult with Charles; rather, he told Charles what he intended to do, and he didn't mention the name of his bride-to-be. Charles wrote in his diary, "I was thunderstruck." A few days later when he learned who the woman was, Charles "retired to mourn." He "groaned all the day, and several following ones, under my own and for the people's burden. I could eat no pleasant food, nor preach, nor rest either by night or by day."

Despite his inner turmoil, he dared not intervene this time.

John wasn't going to let a courtship interfere with his preaching schedule, and it didn't slow him down one bit until a fortuitous accident. Crossing London Bridge in mid-February 1751, he slipped and badly sprained his ankle. Despite the pain, he preached on schedule in the afternoon and then hobbled to the home of Widow Vazeille, his fiancée. Molly acted as his nurse for the rest of the week. At her home, he spent the time "partly in prayer, reading and conversation, partly in writing an *Hebrew Grammar* and *Lessons for Children*."

The conversation with Molly must have settled some things about their marriage. Wesley wanted to make sure that Molly knew he would never touch a penny of her fortune. At least one of her four children was strongly opposed to the marriage, and John probably wanted to remove any suspicion that he was marrying her for her money. No doubt, he also informed her about his evangelistic missions, which kept him away from home 75 percent of the time. She would have her choice of accompanying him on his arduous trips or staying home with her family.

John probably told her, as he had told others, that no Methodist preacher, least of all himself, should "preach one sermon or travel one day less in a married than in a single state." What this meant, of course, was that John would not be making any adjustments to married life; Molly would have to make the adjustments.

The following Monday, his sprained ankle notwithstanding, John and Molly were married. The previous day, Sunday, he had preached on his knees, because he was not able to stand on his sprained ankle. On Tuesday, he was preaching again, once again on his knees. In between he sandwiched in the wedding, and presumably he was married on his knees. We don't know much about his wedding, because he neglected to mention it in his journal.

It was a short courtship, perhaps only sixteen days. And undeniably, it was marriage on the rebound, for John was still smarting from the loss of Grace.

Yet at forty-seven, John had a need to be married. He had always enjoyed feminine companionship, and being attractive to women, he usually had it. But as the Methodist movement grew, he had become more and more isolated in his tower of leadership. Even his brother Charles was now separated from him, separated by the happy marriage that Charles had with Sally Gwynne and separated by Charles' rash action in breaking up John's relationship with Grace. So although he met thousands of people a year and knew hundreds as friends, John was a lonely man at times, and when illness or accident confined him to bed, he was at his loneliest. It was while recuperating that he had fallen in love with Grace. This time he had been confined with a sprained ankle in Molly Vazeille's home on Threadneedle Street in London. The conversation which he enjoyed with Molly in those days of convalescence was delightful. In his words, she gave him "all the assurances which words could give, of the most intense and inviolable affection."

Molly Goldhawk Vazeille Wesley, forty-one, had been a servant girl before marrying a London merchant "who had pampered and indulged her." She had become accustomed to a settled middle-class family life. She had four children, the youngest under five years old. John spoke of her having a "middling understanding," and one biographer speaks of her as being "no more than conventionally religious." Wesley's early biographers denigrated Molly and exonerated John, so some of the early comments on Molly's character may be biased.

Some of these early biographers think that by marrying John, Molly was climbing the social ladder of middle-class respectability and that she inveigled him into marriage, something that Grace Murray and Sophy Hopkey had been unable to do. That is too crass an assessment. Two of her late husband's friends had recommended John Wesley to her. She was flattered by his attention, just as he was pleased with hers. Both of them were ripe for marriage.

The marriage started poorly and went downhill from there. The Sunday after the wedding, John felt he had to explain to his fellow Methodists why he had married so suddenly and had not consulted with his brethren in advance. The explanation confused his brethren and incensed Molly. He spoke of marriage as "a cross that he had taken up" for their sakes and that he had married to "break down the prejudice about the world and him."

Molly was dumbfounded. Was this the man that she had married?

A week later John was off to a conference, then home for a week and then off again on a long road trip in the north. His first day out he scribbled in his diary, "In respect of travelling abroad, the

Methodist preacher who has a wife should be as though he had none." But at night he wrote a warm letter home to Molly, "You have surely a right to every proof of love I can give, and to all the little help which is in my power. For you have given me even your own self. O how can we praise God enough for making us help meet for each other."

John even wrote to his friend Blackwell the banker and asked him to look out for Molly in his absence: "She has many trials; but not one more than God knows and knows to be profitable to her."

Among her trials was John himself. Molly had already gone to Blackwell and complained about her husband's lack of sensitivity to her needs. Then she went to Charles Wesley, only four months after the wedding. It took courage for her to approach Charles because she knew how strongly he had disapproved of the wedding. He agreed to talk to John privately about the problems and then have a meeting among the three of them to engineer a reconciliation. The meeting accomplished little. Molly listed all of the faults, not only of John but also of Charles; John insisted that he couldn't halt his God-given ministry in order to coddle Molly; and Charles felt called upon to re-cite Latin poetry to calm the waters.

Charles never got along with his sister-in-law. "I must pray or sink into a spirit of revenge," he said after enduring one of Molly's seasons of complaint and insult. Charles' negative feelings were contagious and infected other Methodist leaders. Molly was starting to feel paranoid; she was the wife of the leader of Methodism and yet everyone was against her.

Molly had tried one alternative — staying home while John was on the road — and it hadn't worked. Now she was ready to try the other. If she traveled with her husband, maybe the marriage bond would be strengthened and the negative vibes that she was feeling would disappear.

But it didn't work. Grace Murray had been an ideal traveling companion for John; Molly was not. He didn't want to make the comparison, but he couldn't help it. England's roads were not easy to travel, especially the way John Wesley traveled them. And for one who had a penchant for complaining, Molly found she had plenty to bemoan.

Once again John wrote to his confidant Blackwell: "In my last journey all my patience was put to the proof again and again. I am content with whatever I meet with and this must be the spirit of all who take journeys with me. I never fret. I repine at nothing. I am discontented with nothing. And to have persons at my ear, fretting and murmuring at everything is like tearing the flesh off my bones."

Besides the grueling travel schedule, Molly had to face pouring rain, driving winds, winter cold, stones thrown by angry mobs, and taunts of jeering antagonists. Once, when she arrived at the site of the next meeting, she and John were met by a bevy of adoring women all arrayed in "remarkable neatness." She was conscious of two things: first, that she looked her worst after a fifty-mile ride on horseback and second, that the women were gathered around her husband and didn't care a bit about her. After the meeting, while John was exulting about spiritual blessings, she was complaining about the hard beds, the itchy bed covers that were too small, and the crawly little bugs.

It was no doubt after circumstances like that, that Molly's hair-pulling story took place, if indeed it did take place. According to one of Methodism's traveling preachers: "Once when I was in the north of Ireland, I went into a room and found Mrs. Wesley foaming with fury. Her husband was on the floor, where she had been trailing him by the hair of his head. She herself was still holding in her hand venerable locks which she had plucked up by the roots." Allegedly, this took place about a year and a half after their marriage.

Later biographies partially discredit the story, though they don't discredit it completely. Molly's temper was legendary, and when she lost it, she became quite irrational. John once wrote, in the impersonal way by which he sometimes referred to his wife, "It is a pity. I should be glad if I had to do with reasonable people."

There were occasional respites and at first, John's letters show love and affection. He appreciated her assistance with business and financial matters. He even naively encouraged her to open any letters that came to their home while he was traveling. And when Molly opened some of his mail, it started her off on another tantrum.

The problem was that John's intimate counseling of women did not change after his marriage. He was as warm, loving, and solicitous as ever. So after John and Molly mutually agreed that Methodism's best interests weren't served by her traveling with her husband across the British Isles, she stayed at home, read John's mail, and imagined the worst.

Sarah Ryan, a recent convert and only thirty-three years old, had been appointed by John to be matron of the Kingswood School. She had been married three times without benefit of divorce, and was certainly not the people's choice for the coveted post.

Wesley gave her his pastoral counsel. In his letters to her, he told her his problems with Molly, and the language he used to speak of his spiritual interest in her could easily have been misunderstood. And it was.

In return, Sarah's letters to John said things like: "I do not know how to steer between extremes, of regarding you too little or too much." When Molly ripped open one of these letters, she obviously thought it was too much. What John viewed as *agape* love seemed suspiciously like *eros* love to Molly. She demanded that John stop the correspondence.

"I afterwards found her in such a temper," John writes, "as I have not seen her in several years." And then Molly walked out on him, "vowing she would see me no more."

The temper tantrum and Molly's departure didn't stop John from writing to his female lieutenant at Kingswood. A month later, however, at a meeting that Wesley had with more than sixty of his Methodist ministers and with Sarah Ryan presiding, Molly burst into the room, waving her finger at Sarah and shouting, "The whore now serving you has three husbands living."

After that explosion, Molly returned to John, but as you can imagine, life wasn't any easier. At times, the relationship resembled a pitched battle. Molly was the violent one, John the self-righteous. She accused him of having his brother's wife as a mistress. He accused her of poisoning the minds of the servants against him.

When she refused to give him some of the letters that had arrived in his absence, he broke into her bureau forcibly to retrieve them. When she felt the whole world was on John's side and no one understood her predicament, she doctored some of John's letters to cast them in the worst possible light and then gave them to the London newspapers to publish.

Ebenezer Blackwell, who frequently tried to mediate in the marriage, was sometimes caught in the crossfire. He tried to get John to see that all the blame should not be placed upon Molly. John was angry. He responded: "What I am is not the question, but what she is, of which I must needs be a better judge than you." And "I certainly will, as long as I can hold a pen, assert my right of conversing with whom I please. Reconciliation or none, let her look to that."

In one letter to Molly, John listed ten major complaints, including Molly's stealing from his bureau, his inability to invite friends in for tea, her making him feel like a prisoner in his own house, his having to give an account to Molly of everywhere he went, Molly showing his private papers and letters without his permission, her use of fishwife's language against the servants, and her continual malicious slander.

He vowed that he would be willing to do anything to keep her "in good humor," as long as it didn't hurt his soul or hers or the cause of God. Writing his warm letters to Sarah Ryan and other women was necessary to the "cause of God."

Naturally, John had a problem appearing in public with Molly because he was never quite sure what she would say. He writes that she "could not refrain from throwing squibs" at him and would speak to him as "no wife ought to speak to a husband."

"You violently shock my love," he wrote to her. "You cut yourself off from joint prayer. For how can I pray with one that is daily watching to do me hurt. O Molly, throw the fire out of your bosom."

Molly's problems multiplied. Continually, she

was put down by others in the Methodist movement; she wasn't the wife she ought to be for John and she knew it. She was constantly reminded of it. She didn't have John's education, social standing, or stamina; she wasn't suited to be a leader of the Methodist women's bands.

She knew she had an acid tongue. However, not all the blame for their unhappy marriage was hers, and she wanted the world to know it.

She resented the pastoral letters she received from her husband, as if she were no nearer and dearer to him than Sarah Ryan. John would write her: "How do you look back on your past sins?" And "If you were buried just now, or if you had never lived, what loss would it be to the cause of God?" She didn't like to be preached at by her husband.

Besides that, her health was poor. She suffered painfully from gout and had a difficult time going through menopause. She had been defrauded of much of her inheritance and her children had been a concern to her. One had died, another was sickly, and two of her sons proved to be "grievous crosses." John wrote her about these personal problems, suggesting that perhaps these afflictions had come from God "to break the impetuosity and soften the hardness" of her heart. She admitted to herself that this might be so, but she wished that her husband didn't have to keep reminding her.

John Wesley pleaded with her, lectured her and, when that didn't work, he ignored her. John could persuade most women, but he was unable to budge Molly. "One might as well try to convince the north wind," he said.

For more than twenty years, the Wesleys' "marital history pursued its thorny course," writes Stanley Ayling. "A marriage largely nominal and often almost irrelevant; separation frequent, but never final until 1776; perennial mutual resentment."

Sometimes there was a short period of togetherness as in 1766 when Wesley, now sixty-three, wrote, "My wife continues in an amazing temper. Miracles are not ceased. Not one jarring string. O let us live now."

But four years later, on what was almost their twentieth anniversary, Molly walked out again; Wesley's journal records it: "January 23. For what cause I know not, my wife set out for Newcastle, purposing never to return. 'Non eam reliqui; non dimisi; non revocabo.' " ('I have not left her; I have not sent her away; I shall not ask her to come back.')

A year later she came back on her own. Not only did she come back, but she also traveled with him on one of his speaking tours. She was sixty-two at the time.

As they traveled, she felt the strong antagonism of Methodist leadership against her. She felt that they were placing John on a pedestal and her in the gutter. In 1774 she wrote her husband, "For God's sake, for your sake, put a stop to this torrent of evil that is poured out against me."

The torrent did not stop. In 1776 (when he was seventy-three and she sixty-seven) they separated for the last time. "The water is spilt," John wrote. "And it cannot be gathered up again."

Two years later, he wrote her his last letter. It was bitter. "If you were to live a thousand years, you could not undo the mischief you have done."

In 1781, at the age of seventy-two, Molly Vazeille Wesley died. She bequeathed nothing to John except her ring. According to the will, the ring was left as a "token that I die in love and friendship towards him."

John Wesley continued his almost herculean labors. He crossed the Irish Sea forty-two times. When he was eighty he conducted a mission tour in Holland. His bitterness against Molly passed away in his final years, and he viewed those stormy years of marriage with the idea that if "Mrs. Wesley had been a better wife," he might have been unfaithful to the great work to which God had called him.

John Wesley was married to his work, and he felt it would have been a grievous sin to be unfaithful to that divine marriage. But sometimes a servant of God fails to distinguish between loving God and loving God's work.

CHAPTER THREE

Meet Jonathan and Sarah Edwards

YOU may remember Jonathan Edwards for three things: (1) he was the preacher of a sermon entitled "Sinners in the Hands of an Angry God," (2) he was a key figure in America's Great Awakening, and (3) he was a brilliant metaphysical philosopher.

None of those things make him a popular folk hero like Johnny Appleseed and none of them give him an inside track on being a good husband.

Maybe he wasn't a particularly good husband; maybe the credit for the good marriage should go to his wife, Sarah.

I'll let you decide that.

In a day when marriages tended to be cold and formal, this one was warm and friendly.

What was it that made this marriage a success?

"A sweeter couple I have not yet seen." That was what Evangelist George Whitefield of England wrote regarding Jonathan and Sarah Edwards.

In fact, after visiting their Massachusetts home for a few days, Whitefield was so impressed with the Edwards' household that he resolved to get married when he returned home to England.

That may sound strange to you. After all, Jonathan Edwards is best known for his fire-and-brimstone sermon, "Sinners in the Hands of an Angry God," in which he says: "The God that holds you over the pit of hell, much as one holds a spider, or some loathsome insect, over the fire, abhors you, and is dreadfully provoked."

Writer Samuel Hopkins visited the Edwards home and had to admire "the perfect harmony and mutual love and esteem that subsisted between them."

Somehow we find it difficult to imagine that Jonathan Edwards could compose one half of such an idyllic marriage. Besides being a revivalist and a theologian, Jonathan was also one of the greatest philosophers America has ever produced. He was a profound metaphysical, abstract theoretician. Does that sound like a person from whose home would come harmony, love, and esteem?

To tell the truth, that home produced not only harmony, love, and esteem, but a study of 1,400 descendants of Jonathan and Sarah Edwards indicated that it also produced 13 college presidents, 65 professors, 100 lawyers, 30 judges, 66 physicians, and 80 holders of public office including 3 senators, 3 governors, and a vice president of the United States.

Much, but by no means all, of the credit for the happy union goes to Sarah Edwards. Elisabeth D. Dodds called her book on Sarah Edwards *Marriage to a Difficult Man,* and no doubt he was a difficult man. Lost in his own world, impractical, and moody, Jonathan Edwards must have been a challenge to live with.

To the outsider, Sarah looked as if she was the one who had it all together. She never seemed to lose her composure, except in times of religious revival. She seemed to manage household and family calmly. But Jonathan Edwards knew better, especially once when she seemed on the verge of a nervous breakdown.

It takes two to make a good marriage, and both Jonathan and Sarah spent time making it work. Both of them were fascinating individuals, so let's take a closer look at them.

On the surface, Jonathan Edwards had a lot in common with John Wesley. Both men were born in the same year — 1703. Both were sons of ministers. Both were raised in remote country towns. Both were surrounded by doting sisters. Of course,

Edwards was born in East Windsor, Connecticut, not Epworth, England, and his father was a Congregational minister, not an Anglican rector.

Jonathan Edwards had ten sisters. All of them were tall — so was Jonathan — and the father called them his "sixty feet of daughters."

A precocious child, Jonathan loved nature and God. At thirteen, he wrote an extraordinary essay on "flying spiders." But even earlier than that he and his playmates had built a hut in a nearby swamp, not as a clubhouse, but as a prayer house. "I used to pray five times a day in secret," he wrote much later, "and to spend much time in religious talk with other boys, and used to meet with them in secret to pray together. . . . I with some of my schoolmates joined together and built a booth in a swamp, in a very retired spot, for a place of prayer. And besides, I had a secret place of my own in the woods, where I used to retire by myself."

He entered Yale to study philosophy when only thirteen. Admittedly, Yale wasn't the university that it is today, but without a doubt Edwards wasn't a typical teenager. Writer James Wood says, "Brilliantly gifted, Jonathan Edwards at the age of fifteen to eighteen could have become a scientist, a naturalist or a philosopher, ranging freely over the whole world of thought. He might well have become a major poet."

Instead, he became a theologian. At seventeen, he was converted. The Scripture verse which God used in his life was 1 Timothy 1:17: "Now unto the King, eternal, immortal, invisible, the only wise God, be honour and glory for ever and ever. Amen." That verse boggled Edwards' mind. After confronting that verse, Edwards says, "I began to have a new kind of apprehension and ideas of Christ, and the work of redemption and the glorious way of salvation by Him."

By the time he was nineteen he had his ministerial degree and was off to New York City for a brief pastorate in a Presbyterian church there.

Then he came back to join the faculty of Yale. It was not the best of times for Yale. Bickering, heresy-hunting, and internal dissension rocked the school. While everyone else seemed to be throwing mud, young Edwards frequently found himself trying to run the college. The task was too big for him. His inadequacy weighed him down. He was beset with "despondencies, fears, perplexities, multitudes of cares and distraction of mind," in his own words.

One distraction was thirteen-year-old Sarah Pierrepont, daughter of a prominent New Haven minister who had been a driving force in the founding of Yale. Sarah was seven years younger than Jonathan and totally unlike him. He was moody; she was vibrant. He was shy; she was outgoing. He was socially inept; she was a natural conversationalist. He was gawky; she was graceful.

And she played "hard to get."

On the social ladder, the Pierreponts were top rung. Her mother was a granddaughter of Thomas

Hooker, noted Puritan divine and New Haven's founding father. Though she was only thirteen, suitors were already standing in line. Almost all of them were more dashing, more suave than gangling Jonathan. And since most girls in colonial days were married by the time they were sixteen, Sarah's single days were numbered.

But she couldn't forget Jonathan. She liked nature and so did Jonathan. They walked and talked along the shore. She liked to read, too. One of her books on the nature of the Covenant deeply influenced Jonathan's theological thinking. He seemed to respect her mind; he liked to talk to her about deep things.

Despite all the pressures and distractions at the university, Jonathan usually had no trouble concentrating. But after he met Sarah, things changed. At the strangest times, she intruded into his thoughts. It took discipline to resist the temptations. He wrote: "When I am violently beset with temptation...[I resolve to do some study] which necessarily engages all my thoughts and unavoidably keeps them from wandering." Such as studying Greek grammar, for instance.

Obviously, it didn't always work. On the front page of Jonathan's Greek grammar book was found this ode to Sarah: "They say there is a young lady in New Haven who is beloved of that Great Being, who made and rules the world, and that there are certain seasons in which the Great Being, in some way or another invisible, comes to her and fills her mind with exceeding sweet delight, and that she hardly cares for anything except to meditate on him. . . . She has a strange sweetness in her mind, and singular purity in her affections; is most just and conscientious in all her conduct; and you could not persuade her to do anything wrong or sinful if you would give her all the world. . . . She will sometimes go about from place to place, singing sweetly and seems to be always full of joy and pleasure; and no one knows for what. She loves to be alone, walking in the fields and groves, and seems to have someone invisible always conversing with her."

After three years of friendship and courtship, Jonathan pressed her for marriage with the words: "Patience is commonly esteemed a virtue, but in this case I may almost regard it as a vice."

Choosing the course of virtue, Sarah Pierrepont consented to marry the lanky young man and on July 20, 1727, when he was twenty-three and she was seventeen, they were wed.

They were married for thirty-one years, until death parted them in 1758. Twenty-three of those years were spent in the west-central Massachusetts town of Northampton. Jonathan had been called to take charge of a 600-member parish, stepping into the shoes of his grandfather Solomon Stoddard, who had finally decided to retire at eighty-three. It was the largest and most significant church outside of Boston.

Perhaps the young couple would have been

more suited for a parish in Boston. He was an intellectual, not a frontier preacher. She had come from an aristocratic background and her tastes had been properly cultivated. Yet they felt divinely directed to Northampton.

Jonathan always enjoyed writing more than preaching, so he wrote out all his sermons in the style of the day. His style was certainly not dramatic. According to one biographer, "Tall, slight, round-faced with a high forehead and a student's pallor, he spoke quietly and distinctly. His face was grave, his manner dignified. He used no gestures. He depended for effect on the earnestness of his speech, the clarity of his sentences and the skillful use of the pause." The style was Twentieth-Century Funeral Director.

His sermons, which later became famous, were written on scraps of paper, backs of bills from the general store, backs of his children's writing exercises, and backs of broadside ads. Winslow writes, "Edwards saved scraps of paper just as he saved scraps of time. Both could be made to serve a useful purpose." Today, both sides of Edwards' sermon notes fascinate the historian.

Edwards rose early each day. He noted in his journal, "I think Christ has recommended rising early in the morning by His rising from the grave very early." He had a phobia against wasting time. "Resolved never to lose one moment of time, but to improve it in the most profitable way I can."

But this didn't mean he spent all his time praying and reading his Bible. One hour each day was spent in physical work. Chopping wood was a favorite wintertime chore for him. Sometimes he spent more than that, but Sarah was the manager not only of the household but also of the garden and the fields. Edwards once asked, "Isn't it about time for the hay to be cut?" Sarah responded, "It's been in the barn for two weeks."

Samuel Hopkins wrote: "It was a happy circumstance that he could trust everything to the care of Mrs. Edwards with entire safety and with undoubting confidence. She was a most judicious and faithful mistress of a family, habitually industrious, a sound economist, managing her household affairs with diligence and discretion. While she uniformly paid a becoming deference to her husband and treated him with entire respect, she spared no pains in conforming to his inclination and rendering everything in the family agreeable and pleasant."

Sometimes Hopkins paints a picture of Sarah which is almost too good to be true. Yet when he says that she "conformed to his inclination," he is quite accurate. Edwards occasionally skipped dinner when perplexed by a philosophical or theological problem in his study. At other times he became emotional. "I have had very affecting views of my own sinfulness and vileness; very frequently to such a degree as to hold me in a kind of loud weep-ing so that I have often been forced to shut myself up."

Sarah had to learn to live with that.

Jonathan loved to ride his horse, although he resented the time it took to travel. To make proper use of the time, he wrote notes as he was riding. So that he wouldn't forget his valuable thoughts, he pinned his notes to his coat. When he arrived home, it was Sarah's chore to unpin all the notes and help him sort out the ideas.

To give Sarah some time away from the children, he would frequently go riding with her. It wasn't simply a respite from the cares of the family; it was more the fact that Jonathan enjoyed her companionship. So, about four o'clock in the afternoon, they often went horseback riding together. At such times he would discuss ideas with her and hash over parish problems.

Late at night, when everyone else was tucked in bed, Sarah and Jonathan would share a devotional time together in his study.

The "everyone else" began with a baby girl, born a year after their marriage, and concluded twenty-two years later with the birth of their eleventh child.

"She had an excellent way of governing her children," Samuel Hopkins eulogizes. "She knew how to make them regard and obey her cheerfully, without loud, angry words, much less heavy blows. . . . If any correction was necessary, she did not administer it in a passion. . . . In her directions in matters of importance, she would address herself to the reason of her children, that they might not only know her will, but at the same time be convinced of the reasonableness of it.... Her system of discipline was begun at a very early age and it was her rule to resist the first as well as every subsequent exhibition of temper or disobedience in the child...wisely reflecting that until a child will obey his parents, he can never be brought to obey God."

Jonathan himself set aside an hour at the close of each day to spend with his children. According to Hopkins, the seemingly stern preacher of righteousness "entered freely into the feelings and concerns of his children and relaxed into cheerful and animated conversations, accompanied frequently with sprightly remarks and sallies of wit and humor.... Then he went back to his study for more work before dinner."

A little of Edwards' philosophy about the family is disclosed in his books and sermons. "The whole world of mankind is kept in action from day to day by love." And "Every family ought to be a little church, consecrated to Christ and wholly influenced and governed by His rules. And family education and order are some of the chief means of grace. If these fail, all other means are likely to prove ineffectual."

But despite all that Jonathan may have said about love and joy, it was Sarah who exuded it. When she was gone from the house for a few days, one of Edwards' daughters wrote "all is dark as Egypt."

Visitors came frequently to the Edwards' home and stayed overnight. Usually they were more affected by the character of the home than by anything that Jonathan Edwards may have said to them in conversation.

One visitor named Joseph Emerson commented: "The most agreeable family I was ever acquainted with. Much of the presence of God here."

The first time Hopkins visited, Jonathan Edwards wasn't home. "I was very gloomy," Hopkins recalled, "and was most of the time retired in my chamber." Sarah eventually interrupted and asked about his moodiness. He responded by admitting that he "was in the Christless graceless state," and she talked with him about how he could find the spiritual help he needed. When Jonathan returned, there was more conversation. This combination of Sarah's personal interest, the family atmosphere, and Jonathan's theological explanations changed the course of Hopkins' life.

In 1734, the Great Awakening began in Northampton's church after Edwards had preached a series of expository sermons on love from 1 Corinthians 13. "Scarcely a single person in the whole town was left unconcerned about the great things of the eternal world," said Edwards. He was only thirty-one; Sarah (with four daughters by that time) only twenty-four, and they felt they had a tiger by the tail. Emotions were running wild. Even Sarah herself was caught up in ecstasy. The parsonage had become the most popular place in town. Skeptics who investigated were converted. Edwards tried to impose ground rules to control emotional outbursts, but he wasn't always successful. Some three hundred people claimed to have been converted in the small Massachusetts town during a six-month period.

Just as quickly as it had exploded, it faded away. Then came the letdown. Many of the townspeople who claimed a spiritual experience returned to their old vices. Jonathan was discouraged. What amazed him, however, is what he began to observe happening in Sarah. Normally the cool, calm manager, she began to be irritable, finicky, picky. Looking back on this period in her life, Jonathan later wrote that she was "subject to unsteadiness and many ups and downs . . . often subject to melancholy. She had," uncharacteristically for her, "a disposition to censure and condemn others."

Of course, an outsider like Hopkins didn't detect any change at first. "She made it a rule to speak well of all," he wrote and lauded her patience, cheerfulness, and good humor. Jonathan knew better.

Opposition to Jonathan Edwards had begun to build in Northampton, and Sarah didn't know how to cope with it. She had always been popular with everyone; she had no enemies, and wouldn't know what to do if she had them. Jonathan, however, had plenty of foes. Even some of his cousins were making life miserable for him. Sometimes he didn't sense the opposition as soon as Sarah did. He stayed in his study. She would be out on the streets, in the shops, meeting people. Clouds were gathering around Northampton. Sarah could often feel what Jonathan could not yet see. She didn't want to disturb him about some of the petty problems in his parish. So she tried to keep up a good front; underneath, however, it was becoming more and more difficult for her to handle.

Sarah was only thirty, but she had already been the lady of the manse for thirteen years when 1740 rolled around. And in the next two years, more seemed to happen than in the previous thirteen.

She had just given birth to her seventh child (and sixth daughter). Four days later, she was shaken by the news that her older sister had died. That spring there was more illness than usual among the children and the financial needs of the Edwards' household became critical. No doubt urged by Sarah, Jonathan went to the town council to ask for a raise in pay.

That fall, twenty-six-year-old evangelist George Whitefield came to town. He had already stirred up Philadelphia and Boston; Northampton, which had experienced an awakening five years earlier, was ripe for another one. So was Sarah. Her heart, she said, "was swallowed up in a kind of glow of Christ's love coming down as a constant stream of sweet light."

No less stirred was Whitefield himself. He was deeply impressed with the Edwards' children, with Jonathan ("I have not seen his Fellow in all New England"), and especially Sarah. He was moved by her ability to talk "feelingly and solidly of the things of God." He was amazed at how much of a helpmeet she was for her husband. Because of Sarah he renewed his prayers for a wife. He was married the following year.

If the Revival of 1735 was Phase One of the Great Awakening, the spark kindled by Whitefield in 1740 was Phase Two. In New England, it was Jonathan Edwards who kept fanning the flames. Though by style and inclination he was an unlikely revivalist, he was called away from home for weeks at a time to conduct evangelistic services in other New England churches. It was during this time that his sermon "Sinners in the Hands of an Angry God" became famous.

During this time, Sarah was once again struggling with her inner stability. She didn't like it when her husband was away from home so much, and yet she knew she couldn't ask him to stay in Northampton. God was using him wherever he went.

Jonathan didn't accept all the invitations that came his way. Some he turned down saying, "I have lately been so much gone from my people." But in mid-January 1742, in one of the most severe winters of the eighteenth century, he was going away again, and Sarah as usual was left home with her seven children. Every even-numbered year since their wedding, a baby had been born in the Edwards' home. In 1742, Sarah wasn't pregnant. "I felt very uneasy and unhappy. . . . I thought I very much needed help from God. . . . I had for some time been earnestly wrestling with God."

Just before Jonathan had left, he had criticized her for being too negative about a "Mr. Williams of Hadley" who had been preaching in Northampton. Her husband's criticism came when she was very vulnerable. She crumbled. "It seemed to bereave me of the quietness and calm of my mind not to have the good opinion of my husband." Not only was she afraid that she had lost the confidence of her husband but she also feared that she had offended Williams.

In Jonathan's absence from town, a recent seminary graduate named Samuel Buell came to the church to preach. Sarah was emotionally down. Of course, she wanted the revival fires to burn through his preaching; yet she feared that Buell might prove to be a better preacher than her husband and in the process show Jonathan up.

Did she want revival to come back to Northampton even if it meant someone other than Jonathan would be God's instrument? Especially if it meant a flashy young preacher like Samuel Buell? It was difficult for Sarah; she struggled for spiritual victory over it. But at length she attended Buell's sermons and "rejoiced" at the "greater success attending his preaching than had followed the preaching of Mr. Edwards."

And then once again Sarah was encompassed with feelings of ecstasy. Her "soul dwelt on high, was lost in God and almost seemed to leave the body." Hymns ran through her mind and she had a difficult time to "refrain from rising from my seat and leaping for joy."

The next day she fainted from exhaustion in the middle of the day, and she "lay for a considerable time faint with joy." During the following days, she says that she had a "sense of the infinite beauty and amiableness of Christ's person, and the heavenly sweetness of his transcendent love." She emerged from the time a renewed peson. "I never felt such an entire emptiness of self-love, or any regard to any private selfish interests of my own. I felt that the opinions of the world concerning me were nothing." From this time on, she experienced "a wonderful access to God in prayer."

While Sarah no longer regarded "the opinions of the world," she did regard the opinion of her husband. And she was afraid that when he returned and found out what had happened, he might think that she had made a fool of herself. After all, he had been trying to keep emotional excesses out of the revival.

But Jonathan's reaction was sympathetic. He was very interested in her experiences and asked her to describe her emotions as carefully as she could. Like a psychologist, Edwards took her stream of consciousness down in shorthand. Later, he published this (though anonymously to keep from embarrassing her) as part of a defense of the revival.

He didn't care to use his wife as a guinea pig or to analyze her experience scientifically, but he felt he had to. He had been disappointed in the seemingly short-lived effects of the revival of 1735. Some people had been genuinely converted, but many had only been caught up in emotion. The question was: What would be the long-range result of Sarah's experience?

He didn't glorify emotional religious experiences — even the experiences of his wife. In almost every emotional experience, "there is a mixture of that which is natural, and that which is corrupt, with that which is divine."

Jonathan, who had observed certain changes in Sarah's cool and collected self in the previous two or three years, could have guessed that Sarah would soon have to have some emotional release for what she had kept bottled up. So part of her experience was natural, but another part of it was undeniably spiritual.

She had been converted as a child; Jonathan knew that. She had lived a good life; Jonathan knew that too. He also knew that this experience was not only emotional; it was also spiritual. Sarah had her thoughts focused on Jesus Christ.

A year later Jonathan wrote up the results of his

scientific study. Sarah now had an assurance of God's favor that she didn't have before. She was at rest with herself as well as with God. Jonathan was amazed at her "constant sweet peace, calm and serenity of soul." Whatever she did, she was now doing for the glory of God, not for the admiration of men. In Edwards' words, she lived with a "daily sensible doing and suffering everything for God." To him, the "daily sensible doing" was the bottom line of religious revival.

Perhaps, without such a spiritual experience, Sarah couldn't have handled the coming problems in Northampton.

The first problem was finances. Northampton had been growing increasingly unhappy with the need in the Edwards' family for more funds. On the one hand, both Sarah and Jonathan were quite frugal. They saved everything. On the other hand, Sarah had been raised in one of the finest homes in New Haven and it showed. She was accustomed to go "first class." She dressed well and furnished the home in taste. The townspeople didn't understand why Jonathan needed to acquire so many new books. Why couldn't he be content with a few old commentaries? After all, he was preaching from the Bible, wasn't he? The fact that every two years there was another mouth to feed in the Edwards' home didn't get much sympathy. Many families in the area were able to feed several more children on half as much income. History records "a great uneasiness in the town" about the way the Edwards family handled their finances. Finally, Sarah Edwards was asked to turn over the itemized family budget so that everyone could see exactly how they were spending their money.

Why in the world, asked the townspeople, did Jonathan need two wigs? Why did he spend eleven pounds to buy his wife a gold chain and locket? How did Sarah have the nerve to wear such a display of ostentation?

The town was aghast at the extravagance. How could Jonathan ask for more money from the poor church members who were eating off wooden trenchers while he and Sarah and the children were eating from pewter dishes? Jonathan could afford silver buckles on his black shoes, while most of his parishioners had to tie their shoes with common string. And it was obvious to all that Sarah's dresses were expensive.

The financial matter had been a petty irritant for years. When revivals occurred, it was put on the back burner for a while; but the problem was always simmering.

The other problem was that Jonathan had decided not to accept the "non-committed" into church membership. He had discussed it with Sarah and both realized that this would be a major issue. Sarah reported that he "told me that he would not dare ever to admit another person without a profession of real saving religion and spake much of the great difficulties that he expected would come upon him by reason of his opinion."

Why was it such a bone of contention? Because he would be reversing the practice begun by his beloved grandfather, Solomon Stoddard, who had been pastor of the church for more than fifty years. Edwards predicted that, as a result of this decision to reverse his grandfather's procedure, he would be "thrown out of business" and he and his family would be brought to poverty.

Yet Jonathan had to see it through. A college invited him to be its president. Its committee suggested: "You had better run away from these difficulties." According to Sarah: "Mr. Edwards replied that he must not run away."

If the years 1735–1740 were the troubled years for Sarah, the years 1745–1750 were Jonathan's bugbear. Most of his life he had bouts with headaches, colitis, and moodiness. Now he showed his irritation on insignificant matters in the church; even some of his supporters lost heart. A few years later Jonathan mused: "God does not call us to have our spirits ceaselessly engaged in opposition and stirred in anger unless it be on some important occasions." But the issue of a "committed" church membership was important.

In the middle of the unrest, Sarah was asked to go to Boston and take care of an elderly relative who had suffered a stroke. After she had been there a few weeks, Jonathan wrote her tenderly, addressing her as "My dear companion," and told her how the younger children were faring in her absence. Then, after requesting she bring some cheese with her from Boston, he concluded with the line, "We have been without you almost as long as we know how to be."

He often spoke of her as his companion and never did he need a companion more.

In 1750, there were problems aplenty. Sarah had just given birth to her eleventh child and two months later, physically and emotionally depleted, she was flattened by rheumatic fever. That spring, townspeople shunned the Edwards family, refusing to talk with them on the street. Church attendance was only a fraction of what it used to be. A petition was circulated and 200 church members signed it asking for Edwards' dismissal as minister. By mid-year Jonathan was unemployed.

After twenty-three years in Northampton, Jonathan, forty-six, and Sarah, forty, had to move on. The citizens of Northampton, said Paul Elmer More in the *Cambridge History of American Literature*, "had ousted the greatest theologian and philosopher yet produced in this country."

As strange as it may seem, it wasn't easy for Edwards to find another church — or another job of any kind. He was depressed and felt he was over the hill. "I am now thrown upon the wide ocean of the world and know not what will become of me and my numerous and chargeable family." He admitted that he was "fitted for no other business but study."

Northampton, too, had its problems. It couldn't find a minister to fill the shoes of Edwards. For a while, Jonathan filled the pulpit of the church which had boisterously evicted him. He preached without bitterness. Meanwhile Sarah and her daughters made lacework and embroidery and painted fans, which they sent to market in Boston. Those were not easy months for either Jonathan or Sarah.

Then a call came for the distinguished Jonathan Edwards to be a missionary to the Indians in Stockbridge on the western frontier of Massachusetts. There was a small church there. The congregation, composed of several white families and forty-two Indians, was summoned to services by an Indian named David who "blew a blast with a conch shell."

It was a far cry from fashionable New Haven and even from Northampton, the largest church congregation outside of Boston. In primitive Stockbridge, Jonathan preached in a small stuffy room through an interpreter to a small congregation, mostly of Indians who had covered themselves in bear grease as a protection against the winter cold.

Writing to his elderly father in Windsor, Jonathan explained: "My wife and children are well pleased with our present situation. They like the place much better than they expected. Here, at present, we live in peace: which has of long time been an unusual thing with us. The Indians seem much pleased with my family, especially my wife."

Sarah must have wondered about the Lord's leading. Why would He take a scholar like Jonathan and bury him on the frontier? For that matter, why would He take a woman accustomed to the finer things of life and place her in a log cabin surrounded by wigwams?

Actually, Jonathan didn't mind living in isolation from the civilized world. Having a smaller congregation gave him time to do some serious writing. His most famous piece of philosophical writing, *On the Freedom of the Will,* was written in Stockbridge.

Yet it was frustrating to both of them. Jonathan felt inadequate in preaching through an interpreter. He tried to gear his sermons to the level of the Indians, but he realized that there was both a language barrier and a culture barrier between them. Sarah, whose sons and daughters were marrying, found that her interests and concerns were not as much on the ministry at Stockbridge as they ought to be. In Northampton, she had had a ministry of hospitality; the Edwards' home had practically become a hotel. In Stockbridge, not too many New Englanders came calling.

But you couldn't say that things were boring, especially when the French and Indian War started heating up in 1754. Jonathan's mission work was virtually halted. In his congregation had been Mohicans, Mohawks, Iroquois, and Housatonnuck Indians. Some of the Indians favored the French; some the British; and some were on the warpath against both.

Several whites were murdered nearby and soon

the Edwards' home was turned into a little fort. For three years, the Edwards lived in a state of siege. White settlers came from miles away to camp at the compound and four soldiers quartered themselves in the Edwards' house. Later, Sarah submitted a bill to the colonial government for 800 dinners and seven gallons of rum.

Daughter Esther, who had married a young college president named Aaron Burr, returned to Stockbridge to visit her parents during this siege and had trouble getting away again. But while there, she talked to her father about some spiritual problems she was having. "I opened my difficulties and he, as he freely advised and directed the conversation, has removed some distressing doubts that discouraged me much in my Christian warfare. He gave me some excellent directions to be observed in secret that tend to keep the soul near to God as well as others to be observed in a more public way. Oh, what a mercy that I have such a father — such a guide."

It's hardly the picture that most people have of Jonathan Edwards.

The school that Esther's husband served as president was the College of New Jersey, a school that would soon play a part in Jonathan's future. Esther's infant son was named Aaron after his father, and he would play a part — albeit infamously — in America's future.

The French and Indian War finally cooled down, the Indians were returning peacefully to

Stockbridge, and Jonathan and Sarah were ready to resume their missionary ministry, when suddenly they received word that their son-in-law, Aaron Burr, had died.

Five days later, another message came to Stockbridge. The board of directors of the school, which later became better known as Princeton University, had extended an invitation to Jonathan Edwards to replace his son-in-law as president.

Jonathan didn't think he should take the job. Things were just returning to normal in Stockbridge; besides, he had two books on the drawing board that he wanted to finish. Physically and emotionally, he wasn't up to it. "I have a constitution," he wrote back, "in many respects peculiarly unhappy, attended with flaccid solids, vapid... fluids, and a low tide of spirits; often occasioning a kind of childish weakness and contemptibleness of speech, presence, and demeanor, with a disagreeable dulness and stiffness, much unfitting me for conversation, but more especially for the government of a college."

And if that didn't rule him out of further consideration, he admitted that he didn't know algebra and he was not very familiar with the Greek classics. Knowing that a president's job entails much public speaking, he added, "I think I can write better than I can speak."

Princeton's board of trustees was not deterred. They understood his reply to be a "Maybe" rather than a "No," and sent a delegation to Stockbridge to convince the local church council that Edwards was needed in New Jersey more than in Massachusetts' Wild West. Edwards was amazed that his own church council agreed.

So in January 1758, Jonathan left Stockbridge for New Jersey and was inducted as president the following month. His wife, Sarah, would be coming shortly as soon as she was able to conclude the family's affairs in Stockbridge.

But in March, after a presidency of only a few weeks, Jonathan Edwards was stricken with smallpox. As he lay dying, he talked much about his wife and children: "Give my kindest love," he said, "to my dear wife and tell her that the uncommon union that has so long subsisted between us has been of such a nature as I trust is spiritual and therefore will continue forever. And I hope she will be supported under so great a trial and submit cheerfully to the will of God. And as to my children, you are now like to be left fatherless, which I hope will be an inducement to you to seek a Father who will never fail you."

Just before he died, he told one of his daughters who was at his bedside, "Trust in God and you do not need to be afraid."

Sarah, of course, was stunned by the news. What was God's purpose in the call to Princeton? Yet, as Hopkins reported, she "had those invisible supports that enabled her to trust in God."

Two weeks after Jonathan's death, she wrote to one of her children: "My very dear child: What shall I say? A holy and good God has covered us with a dark cloud. . . . He has made me adore His goodness that we had him so long, but my God lives, and He has my heart."

After thirty-one years of marriage, Sarah was separated from her husband by death. Her favorite verse of Scripture came to mean much more to her at this time: "Who shall separate us from the love of Christ? . . . For I am persuaded that neither death nor life . . . nor any other creature shall be able to separate us from the love of God, which is in Christ Jesus our Lord."

Six months later, just as suddenly as her husband had died, Sarah became violently ill with dysentery and died. She was forty-eight.

It had been, as Jonathan Edwards said on his deathbed, a most "uncommon union." One biographer called it "a rare companionship with rich happiness." As companions together, they took time for each other and made their marriage a success. They enjoyed each other's companionship and respected each other's gifts.

Biographers tend to praise Sarah for making the marriage so successful. Perhaps so. But Jonathan shared his ministry with her and thus gave her a larger role than many women of that time enjoyed.

It was an uncommon union indeed.

CHAPTER FOUR

Meet Dwight and Emma Moody

MANY of you know Dwight L. Moody, the Billy Graham of the nineteenth century. An amazing, seemingly tireless evangelist, he crisscrossed the Atlantic winning hundreds of thousands for Jesus Christ.

Yes, you probably know Dwight L. Moody, but I don't think you've ever heard of Emma Moody, his wife, who liked to stay in the background.

I think you should get to know both of them better. You might be surprised at the kind of man Dwight was at home; you might also be surprised at Emma. Just when you think you have her pegged, you find something about her that amazes you.

But what kind of a marriage would this be — between this Martin Lutherlike man and this "shy and reserved" woman? You might be surprised at that, too.

Do opposites attract?

Can a marriage succeed between people who are so different?

When you get to know Dwight and Emma, you'll discover the answers.

"The only person in all the world who really knew D. L. Moody was his wife," writes Biographer J. C. Pollock.

Maybe that's true, but it is doubtful if anyone — even D. L. Moody himself — really knew Emma Moody.

DL (he seldom used his given name Dwight Lyman) and Emma were opposites. In fact, their son Paul said, "No two people were ever more in contrast. . . . He was impulsive, outspoken, dominant, informal and with little education at the time they met. She was intensely conventional and conservative, far better educated, fond of reading, with a discriminating taste, and self-effacing to the last degree."

It was a good thing that they were different. No home would have been big enough for two people like D. L. Moody.

But don't get the idea that Emma Moody was a pushover. She had a mind of her own.

D. L. Moody never put her in her place; she made a place for herself. It was a behind-the-scenes place that she enjoyed, out of the limelight. For instance, she refused to appear on the platform during her husband's evangelistic campaigns — and she faced criticism for it. Yet early in his evangelistic meetings, she was his prize worker in the inquiry room. "When I have an especially hard case," DL once said, "I turn him over to my wife. She can bring a man to a decision for Christ where I cannot touch him." One of Moody's most famous converts, E. P. Brown, a magazine editor and notorious infidel, was led to Jesus Christ by "shy and reserved" Emma Moody.

Moody's accomplishments as an evangelist on both sides of the Atlantic are legendary. He traveled a million miles, preached to a hundred million people and saw 750,000 respond to a gospel invitation. He revolutionized mass evangelism and founded what is known today as the Moody Bible Institute, the first Bible school of its kind.

A big man, five-ten and more than 250 pounds, he grew bigger and broader over the years of his ministry, not merely in physical size but in the scope and character of his ministry. Emma had a lot to do with that.

Born in Northfield, Massachusetts, in 1837, Dwight Moody had no easy time of it. His father, a whiskey-drinking, shiftless stone-mason, died bankrupt when Dwight was only four. Betsey Moody was left with nine children, including Dwight.

In Northfield, Dwight was exposed to little schooling, little Bible instruction, but lots of hard work. At the age of seventeen, Dwight had his fill of the toil of slow-paced, mundane Northfield and headed for Boston, where he took a job in an uncle's shoe store. He slept in the third floor over the shop. He described it in his almost illegible way: "I have a room up in the third story and I can open my winder and there is 3 grat buildings full of girls the handsomest there is in the city they will swar like parrets." His letter also told how he ate his meals at a hostel "where there is about twenty-five clurks and some girls we have a jolly time." Obviously, Dwight liked girls better than punctuation.

For several months he attended Sunday school at the Mount Vernon Congregational Church in Boston. The class was taught by a dry-goods salesman, thirty-year-old Edward Kimball. One day Kimball visited Moody at work in the shoe store and asked the teenager to come to Christ. Moody responded.

However when he applied for church membership a few weeks later, he was turned down. He didn't have a clear understanding of what salvation was all about, they said.

A year later, discouraged by his church and in disagreement with his uncle who employed him, he packed his bags and hopped an immigrant train (fare $5.00) to seek his fortune in Chicago.

The prospects in Chicago excited him. In letters home, he bragged to his mother, "I can make money faster here then I can in B" (meaning Boston), and wrote to his brother George, "Hear is the place to make the money."

Although he was accepted into membership in a Congregational church in Chicago, he also attended Methodist and Baptist churches. He never worried much about denominational labels. While visiting a Baptist mission, he spotted young Emma Revell — not quite fifteen years old. Emma was teaching a class at the Wells Street Mission; Moody was impressed with both the way she taught and the way she looked. Her hair was black, her eyes dark. She was very feminine and almost quaint. There was a certain elegance about her that impressed twenty-year-old Moody, who was anything but elegant.

He was also not a Sunday school teacher. The Baptists wanted to press him into service as a teacher, but he said he couldn't teach. So instead they gave him the job of going out on the streets and "drumming up scholars," a job that DL did extremely well.

He was also quite successful in getting himself invited to the Revell home where he met Emma's father, Fleming Revell, a shipbuilder of French Huguenot roots who had come to Chicago from London only eight years earlier because he had heard a rumor that Chicago had a future as a ship-building center.

DL liked Emma but not her Sunday school. It was too formal; so in 1858 he began his own. At first it met in an abandoned freight car, then in an unused saloon. Within a year, with DL drumming up the scholars, attendance had grown to 600; in another year it hit 1500.

Teaching a class of Moody's ragamuffins was no picnic, but young Emma was one of his first volunteers. There is evidence that DL enjoyed the companionship of all of his female teaching staff, but Emma became increasingly special to him. In his courtship, DL exercised unusual propriety. He normally brought two other men with him to the Revell home. This was partly because Emma had two sisters, but it was also because DL felt a bit out of place in the more formal atmosphere of the Revell home.

In 1860 they were engaged. DL made the announcement at a meeting of his Sunday school teaching staff. It went something like this: "Up until now, I have always walked all of the girls home, but I can't anymore. I'm engaged to Emma Revell."

Those were days of big decisions for DL. In 1859 at the age of twenty-two, he was making $5,000 in commissions on top of his salary as a salesman. That was in a day when mechanics were making $1.50 a day. DL's goal was to make $100,000 a year, and he doubtless would have made it. Henry

Drummond later declared, "There is almost no question that he would have been one of the wealthiest men in the United States."

But DL was starting to lose interest in money. His Sunday school was taking more of his time and attention. In his spare moments he found himself working with the YMCA. Soon it became apparent that he couldn't stay in business and still do a good job with his Sunday school and the YMCA.

For three months he struggled with the decision. "It was a terrible battle," he said. It would mean delaying marriage to Emma. It would mean sleeping on a bench in the prayer room of the Y and eating cheese and crackers in the cheapest restaurants. (And Moody loved to eat.)

But he finally decided to quit his job. He took a position as visitation secretary of the YMCA. If it paid anything at all, it was a pittance. Marriage would have to wait.

At the outbreak of the Civil War, the YMCA set up an army committee, and Moody was sent to minister to the soldiers. He passed out hymn-books — more than 125,000 of them — even though he himself had trouble carrying a tune. He went from barrack to barrack, holding as many as ten meetings a night, although he probably wouldn't have called them meetings.

"I saw the dying men — I heard the groans of the wounded," he recalls. He was criticized by Prohibitionists for giving brandy to dying men in order to revive them, so he could tell them about Jesus.

Sometimes they called him "Crazy Moody," because he was always hurrying somewhere. His uncle said, "My nephew Dwight is crazy, crazy as a March hare." His brother agreed, "Dwight is running from morning to night. He hardly gets time to eat."

In fact, he didn't have time for much of anything. "I do not get five minutes a day to study," he admitted, "so I have to talk just as it happens."

He almost didn't have time to get married. But Emma, now a nineteen-year-old school teacher, was still waiting for him. In his biography of Moody, J. C. Pollock writes, "Emma Revell, who had fallen in love with a prosperous shoe salesman, became engaged to a children's missioner, and was now about to marry a six-horse Jehu, wondered where it would end."

They were married Thursday, August 28, 1862. Dwight Moody was twenty-five.

His mother didn't like the idea of her son marrying a girl who had been born in England and who was also a Baptist. Really, she didn't know which was worse.

DL had, of course, told her of the engagement: "I think, dear Mother, you would love her, if you could get acquainted with her. I do not know of anyone that knows her, but that does. She is a good Christian girl."

Since his mother had responded so negatively to the idea of his engagement to this British Baptist, he decided to take his time about informing her of the marriage. Finally, he got around to it two months later. Her reaction was what he expected.

Emma tackled the challenge with her usual calmness. She wrote her mother-in-law: "It makes very little difference to what sect we belong as long as our hearts are right in the sight of God." It took a few more letters and personal visits but Emma and her mother-in-law, Betsey, soon became close friends.

Emma had a way of handling difficult problems. In fact, DL was sometimes unaware of all she was doing. She was practical and orderly. She made her husband eat regularly. She threw away the patent shirts that he boasted "did not need washing for weeks."

She shunned the limelight although her gifts as a teacher were recognized. In Moody's Sunday school she taught a class of about forty middle-aged men.

Once, Moody was escorting a visitor through his Sunday school, and the visitor remarked about the propriety of the situation: "Isn't that lady too young to be teacher of a class of men like that?"

Moody responded that he thought the teacher was handling the class quite well.

The visitor agreed but still insisted that it seemed improper.

Finally Moody said, and rather proudly at that, "That, sir, is my wife."

In the mid-1860s Moody's Sunday school evolved into a church. DL's closest denominational ties were with the Congregationalists, but his church was independent. At Emma's urging, he included a baptistry for immersion as well as a font for infant baptism.

Moody was never ordained as a minister, so other men became the ministers of his church. Yet this didn't keep him from preaching regularly, and there was no doubt in anyone's mind that it was his church.

In his early sermons he emphasized God's wrath. "I preached that God hated sinners, that He was standing behind sinners with a double-edged sword, ready to cut off the heads of sinners," he recalled later. Even Emma said that she sometimes "cringed" at his remarks.

But then the tone of his sermons changed, and it was Emma who was at least partly responsible. Also responsible was a British preacher named Harry Moorhouse, a converted pickpocket.

Moorhouse had been preaching at Moody's church in DL's absence, and when the evangelist returned, he asked Emma how Moorhouse had handled himself. She replied, "He preaches a little different from you. He preaches that God loves sinners."

Moody couldn't understand what Emma was driving at, but she insisted: "When you hear him, I think you will agree with him. He backs up everything he says with the Bible."

From then on, Moody not only preached more on the love of God than on the wrath of God, but also became more of a Bible student; and his sermons showed it.

Emma was also responsible for DL's ministry in the British Isles. After an unusually severe winter of asthma attacks, Emma, only twenty-four, was urged by her doctor to leave Chicago. He suggested that she might go to England where her older sister lived. Always frail, she suffered from recurring headaches and a heart condition as well as asthma. On the other hand, Moody was robust and seemingly tireless. His chief musician, Ira Sankey, once prayed, "O God, tire Moody out, or give the rest of us superhuman strength."

Moody liked the idea of taking his wife to England. He needed a change of pace himself, and besides, he wanted to meet three men that he had admired from afar: George Williams, head of the YMCA; Charles Spurgeon, preacher at London's Metropolitan Tabernacle; and George Muller, who kept the Bristol Orphanage running by his prayer. Whether the trip to England did much for Emma's health is debatable, but it certainly did a lot to open up a new continent for DL's evangelistic ministry.

Emma may not have met all the dignitaries that her husband met, but she met a few unforgettable characters as well. Once as she was traveling alone by train, she happened to sit in a compartment with an insane man. Said he, "Do you know what

I would have done with my wives if I had been Henry the Eighth?" As he talked, he moved closer to her.

Realizing that she couldn't get out of the compartment, the unflappable Emma responded, "No, tell me."

So he told her, complete with all the blood-curdling details of how women could be slain and hinting that he would like to try some of his ideas on her.

Instead of recoiling, Emma said, "You know, I think I could suggest some ways that you have never even thought of." And she tried to top his methods of torture and execution with a few macabre ones that she thought up on the spur of the moment. Eventually, just as her imagination was becoming exhausted, the train pulled into a station and Emma managed to escape.

The story was not surprising to her friends. They had never seen her flustered, and they doubted if even a maniac would raise her blood pressure.

Perhaps if she could keep calm around D. L. Moody, she could keep calm in any kind of circumstances. Moody was always doing the unexpected, acting on impulses, bringing home unusual visitors, and "surging in and sweeping out," as one biographer stated.

When he paused long enough to consider it, DL marveled at the wife God had given him. Once in a sermon Moody stated, "I think my wife would think it a very strange feeling, if I should tell how much I loved her the first year we were married and how happy I was then. It would break her heart."

Publicly, he said, "I have never ceased to wonder at two things — the use God has made of me despite my many handicaps, and the miracle of having won the love of a woman who is so completely my superior with such a different temperament and background."

By 1871, thirty-three-year-old Moody was very much a family man. Two children had been born into their Chicago home, and some of Moody's rough edges were being smoothed under Emma's gentle sandpapering. At times he was even learning to be courteous. His quick temper was usually kept under control, although occasionally he had to apologize for it in a public meeting.

He was now coming to a crossroads in his career. He had a church in Chicago, a job with the YMCA, and a growing evangelistic ministry that took him away from home for weeks at a time. He felt that God was calling him to more evangelism, but he was resisting.

The Chicago fire burned away his resistance.

On the night of October 8, 1871, the police knocked on the Moodys' door and told them to get out of the area as soon as possible. The city was aflame. Emma calmly wakened her two children and said: "If you promise not to scream or cry, I'll show you a sight you will never forget." She dressed them while they looked out the window at the inferno.

Noticing a neighbor with a horse and wagon, Moody asked if he would take the Moody children to safety. After seeing their children off, DL and Emma packed several Bibles and a few valuables into a baby buggy. Emma tried to get her husband to put a portrait of himself in the baby buggy too. Moody wouldn't think of it. "What would the neighbors say if they saw me pushing a baby buggy down the street with my picture in it?" So Emma carried it herself, under her arm.

For twenty-four hours, DL and Emma didn't know where their children were, or even if they were alive. Emma's jet black hair turned grey overnight.

Chicago was in ashes. So was Moody's church. So was his YMCA. And no longer was there anyone in Chicago from whom he could raise money to build a new church or a new YMCA. So he went to New York and Philadelphia on a fundraising mission. Money came reluctantly.

The problems in raising money to rebuild seemed to verify his call into full-time evangelism, and before long he was headed back to England with Emma, and his two children, Willie, just four, and daughter Emma, now eight. A biographer looking at it psychologically wrote, "When problems began to pile up that were too much for him, he solved these difficulties by getting out and starting anew."

No one in England knew he was coming, except the head of the London YMCA and the doctor at a local lunatic asylum. But the Moodys stayed twenty months and in that time the entire British Isles were set aflame for God.

In Scotland they stayed in the home of Peter Mackinnon, a partner of the British India Line. Mrs. Mackinnon, who became Emma's closest friend, enjoyed both the Moodys. She wrote, "I liked the combination of playfulness and seriousness in Mr. Moody. . . . He is so simple, unaffected and lovable, plays so heartily with the children, and makes fun with those who can receive it. He is brimful of humor."

As for Emma, Jane Mackinnon wrote, "One day was enough to show what a source of strength and comfort she was to her husband. The more I saw of her, the more convinced I was that a great deal of his usefulness was owing to her, not only in the work she did for him, relieving him of all correspondence, but also from her character. Her independence of thought. . .her calmness, meeting so quietly his impulsiveness, her humility. . . . So patient, quiet, bright, humble; one rarely meets just so many qualities in one woman."

Moody's campaigns in the British Isles began with a whimper and ended with a bang. From the tip of Northern Ireland to Cornwall, people were talking about Moody. Emma, in one of her many letters to Moody's mother, talked about him too: "Your son is a gem of a husband."

When the Moodys returned to America, they made their home in Northfield, Massachusetts, where his mother, now in her seventies, still lived. Before long, DL's presence was felt in Northfield.

Concerned about his hometown, Moody prayed for revival there even as he had prayed in London and Glasgow. "The hardest place to begin," he said, "is at home, in your own church, your own family, but that is what God wants us to do."

And that's what Moody did. In the staid Northfield church, he preached one Sunday and saw his own mother stand for prayer. Moody left the platform, sat down in the front pew, his face in his hands, and wept.

Though DL and Emma frequently traveled away from Northfield in the next quarter century, this became their home, and they always longed to get back to it.

The family home in Massachusetts was a beautiful spot, writes James Findlay, Jr., "situated on one of the main roads into Northfield, commanding a sweeping view of the Connecticut River." It was a spacious New England farmhouse, the back portion of which was eventually converted into tiny rooms to serve as a dormitory for Moody's Northfield School.

At home DL relaxed, let his beard grow, wore shabby clothes, puttered in the vegetable garden, and played the role of a gentleman farmer. He loved horses and at one time owned fourteen of them. He cared little for sports and recreation but he enjoyed going out for buggy rides and scaring his passengers out of their wits by the breakneck speeds at which he drove his horses. It was only when Emma was along that he slowed to a respectable speed. He pretended naughtiness and was a "stout and bearded Peter Pan."

Whatever DL did, he did in a big way. When he heard that his mother's chickens had been pecking away in a neighbor's cornfield and the neighbor didn't like it, Moody bought the neighbor's land to keep that problem from recurring. Once when he found himself without a pair of suspenders, he decided to keep that from happening again as well. He went out and bought a gross of suspenders, all white, large-size elastics.

In the homestead, Emma did the canning and made the preserves, visited the neighbors, and entertained DL's friends. She also did most of his correspondence and handled the family finances. DL once declared, "I am not going to give any man ground for saying that we're making a gain out of preaching the gospel." So he turned over the books to Emma.

DL did have a few extravagances. Once he bought a weight-lifting machine which he played with for awhile. He laughed about it later. Indeed, he enjoyed jokes on himself.

Emma managed the house and, in her own quiet

way, the entire family. She took responsibility for the spiritual teaching of their children, catechizing them, memorizing Scripture with them. Though she joined the Congregational Church at Northfield with her husband, she remained a Baptist in her beliefs until her death.

Unlike DL, who didn't read more than he had to, Emma enjoyed reading. As her children were growing up, she studied Latin grammar with them. Later she relearned French.

The one thing that angered Emma was people who took advantage of her husband. A son recalls, "Disloyalty to him was the unpardonable sin in her eyes, unforgivable, unforgettable and above all unmentionable. Here she was implacable."

DL and Emma often took buggy rides together into the woods and hills surrounding their home, and as their son put it, "going where fancy led them, having as it were a renewed honeymoon."

There were times when Moody turned down travel opportunities because "I could not leave my wife." But he did not turn down many opportunities to conduct evangelistic missions. These were often lengthy stays of several months, and usually Emma and the children traveled with him.

Often, they rented a house during the evangelistic missions, but sometimes, they stayed with others. During the Philadelphia campaign they stayed with the Wanamakers. One of the Wanamaker children recalled later, "The thing I remember most was Mr. Moody and father playing bears with us children. Such wild exciting times we had! They could get down on all fours and chase us. We would shriek and scream and run. It was pandemonium." You may be sure, of course, that Emma wouldn't take part in such shenanigans.

Emma wrote to Jane Mackinnon of her daily schedule in the midst of a six-month Baltimore campaign with "Mr. Moody at study and work in the meetings, the children in school, and I in all sorts of work, writing for my husband, attending to some of his calls, and helping him where I can, besides a variety of other things, that don't amount to much and yet make me tired by night."

One of the reasons Emma was getting tired in Baltimore was that she was pregnant. Their third child, Paul Dwight Moody, was born the next spring. He was ten years younger than his older brother, Will.

As the children grew up, both DL and Emma shared a deep concern for them. For instance, when Will began his college work at Yale, DL cautioned him against playing football. "It seems to me like running a great risk of being crippled for life for the sake of a half-hour's fun and exercise," but their greater concern was for the spiritual life of their children. Emma wrote, "If God will only make our children His own, it is the best that we can ask of Him for them." Moody had a special concern because his oldest son, Will, was cool to spiritual matters. Once he wrote Will a revealing letter: "I have not talked much with you for fear I would turn you more and more against Him, who I love more than all the world and if I ever said or done anything unbecoming a Christian father I want you to forgive me. . . . I have always thought that when a mother and father are Christians and their children were not that there was something decidedly wrong with them. I still think so. . . . If I thought I had neglected to do my duty toward my three children I would rather die than live."

Later, it was Emma who wrote to Will about her fear of his "being in college without reliance on the help of Christ. . . . Papa, I know, is praying and I am that God's spirit may lead you to give up yourself to Christ entirely."

The following year Will made a profession of faith. When DL heard of it, he wrote, "I do not think you will ever know until you have a son of your own how much good it did me to hear this."

The younger son, Paul, felt it was easier to confide in his mother than in his father. And Paul gave his mother credit for the success of the home: "If our home seemed so ideal, the secret was my mother."

Emma also deserves some credit for the founding of Moody Bible Institute in Chicago. Moody had served as president of the Chicago Evangelization Society which was planning to launch a training school. But conflict developed between the board of directors and prospective staff members. Moody, who was not on the scene, felt frustrated by the continual bickering. Finally he had enough. He abruptly tendered his resignation as president, a move which would have doomed the entire project. "I am sick and tired of it," he wrote.

When Emma heard about what DL had done, she wrote a nineteen-page letter to the people involved with the Bible Institute, and then got DL to send a wire, withdrawing his resignation.

Soon the Bible Institute of Chicago was launched.

Moody continued his busy schedule, despite his overweight and his advancing age. In one three-month period, he visited ninety-nine places, often speaking three or four times a day. It is said that nothing distressed DL more than idleness.

The year 1899 was difficult for the Moodys. DL was sixty-two and had a full schedule of meetings planned. Two of his grandchildren had died rather suddenly and the parents were suffering emotionally from it. So were the grandparents. DL had been burdened about the city of Philadelphia and had said, "If only it would please God to let me get hold of this city by a winter of meetings. I should like to do it before I die."

So, on his way to an evangelistic campaign in Kansas City, he stopped to visit John Wanamaker in Philadelphia and make final arrangements for a series of revival meetings. He was shocked to find his close friend John Wanamaker living in adultery. He continued to Kansas City, but after two weeks severe chest pains caused him to cease his preaching and he had to return home to

Northfield. A month later, in December 1899, he died.

When DL's body was laid to rest, the spark in Emma's life was gone. She began to fail physically. When neuritis plagued her, she no longer could write with her right hand. So during the last two years of her life she learned to write with her left hand. It was rather typical of the way that Emma Moody handled obstacles.

D. L. Moody once told reporters, "I am the most overestimated person in America." But his wife, he would have said, was the most underestimated. Will Moody once wrote, "Moody found in his wife what he termed his balance wheel. With advice, sympathy and faith, this girl labored with him, and by her judgment, tact and sacrifice, she contributed to his every effort."

An associate of Moody once said, "Only the closest and oldest of his associates knew the extent to which he leaned upon her. She did not intend they should."

Emma supplied what Dwight lacked, and he knew it and appreciated it. She didn't like the limelight; she preferred a behind-the-scenes role. But that doesn't mean she was a nonentity. Far from it. She shaped Dwight both as a man and as a servant of God.

For Dwight, who came from a fatherless home and who didn't know the tenderness of a full family until he met the Revells, it was remarkable that marriage would be so successful. Once again, much credit belongs to Emma.

Dwight needed someone to care for, and Emma, who was physically frail and psychologically strong, was an ideal mate.

In some ways, Dwight was like Martin Luther, impulsive, outspoken and dominant, but with the heart of a teddy bear. But Emma was not a bit like Katie Luther.

Both Martin and Dwight, however, grew in love, appreciation, and respect for the mate God had given. And both Katie and Emma helped shape men who changed the lives of millions.

CHAPTER
FIVE

Meet William and Catherine Booth

WILLIAM BOOTH reached into the dregs of London's society, preached to the down-and-outers, and organized his Salvation Army. Since then, the Army has marched around the world, ministering mercy and preaching the gospel.

His wife, Catherine Booth, is almost as famous as her general-husband. In fact, 100 years ago, it was a moot point who was the better preacher.

How does a marriage work when both husband and wife are public figures? For that matter, when both husband and wife are strong-minded and frequently dogmatic?

At first, you may wonder how this marriage survived, but soon you will see what both William and Catherine brought to it that made it successful.

I think you'll agree that both William and Catherine are fascinating people. You'll enjoy getting to know them.

It was a big day for William, and it turned out to be much bigger than he could possibly have dreamed.

April 10, 1852, was his twenty-third birthday, and this year it coincided with Good Friday. But that wasn't what made it big.

This was the day when William Booth would become a full-time preacher. Up until this day, he had been a seventy-eight-hour-a-week pawnbroker and a Sunday preacher. Now he was saying farewell to the pawnbroker's shop in south London, where he had slept as well as worked for the past three years.

A businessman had promised him $4.00 a week if he would go full time into preaching. It was not an easy decision and he had struggled with it for months. After all, he was trying to send some support to his widowed mother each week, and that would be hard to do on $4.00 a week. But now the decision was made. He had packed his suitcase and had walked out in the street looking for new lodgings.

Then, unexpectedly he bumped into his businessman friend, who invited him to attend a church service that afternoon. Probably if anyone else had given the invitation, William would have refused it; after all, he had other things on his mind.

Instead, he decided to accept the invitation and go to the meeting. He was glad he did.

Catherine Mumford was also attending the meeting.

They had met a few times before. In some ways they seemed an unlikely couple. He was tall (about six-one), almost Lincolnesque in his appearance, gangling, a bit awkward, sporting a black beard and usually wearing a dark frock coat. She was dark, slightly built, had lustrous brown eyes, and carried herself with obvious refinement.

She had become one of his parishioners at the Walworth Road Methodist Chapel where he frequently preached. One biographer says that "despite their brief acquaintance, a strange affinity had grown up between the tall hollow-cheeked Booth and the dark petite Catherine."

And on this Good Friday that was so significant in William Booth's life, he offered to escort her home after the meeting; she accepted.

Earlier she had admired his preaching (it had "fire" in it); now she began to admire the man. "His thought for me, although such a stranger, appeared most remarkable." She was also impressed with the "wonderful harmony of view and aim and feeling on varied matters. It seems as though we had intimately known and loved each other for

131

years. . . . Before we reached my home we both suspected, nay we felt as though we had been made for each other, and that henceforth the current of our lives must flow together."

Catherine's mother invited William to stay at their home for the night. The next morning when he left the Mumford home, he said he was "feeling wounded." William Booth had fallen in love.

Unfortunately, it was not a good time to fall in love. If it had happened a day earlier when he still had his job, everything might have been different. But now he was a preacher, and $4.00 a week was hardly enough to meet his own bare necessities. He certainly couldn't afford to get married.

Had the decisions of this Good Friday been a mistake?

It would be easy to think so. Both William and Catherine were intense, opinionated, strong-minded, determined. Both were frequently moody and prone to depression.

How could such a marriage work out?

But it did.

Booth lived to see the Salvation Army which he and Catherine began in the London slums spread into fifty-five countries. The merger of social concern and aggressive evangelism among all types of people added a refreshing new dimension to Christendom. No religious movement has ever been more the product of a husband-wife team than the Salvation Army. And no family has ever disseminated the gospel farther and more effectively than

William and Catherine Booth and their eight children.

Perhaps their most serious disagreement during their engagement was over women's equality. She won the argument, but a decade later it was her husband who prodded her into preaching, and a decade after that, she was in more demand as a preacher than he was.

Yes, William and Catherine were an unlikely couple, and both of them came from homes with below-par marriages.

"There is no evidence," one biographer avers, "that Mary (William Booth's mother) greatly loved Samuel Booth (his father), or indeed that she loved him at all. His cold nature and worldly ambitions and his vulgar speech and manners must have checked whatever affection she might have felt for him." His father, whom William himself describes as "a grab-a-get," was a money-minded, small-time builder in Nottingham, who tried to keep up appearances as long as possible but went bankrupt in 1842 when William was only thirteen. That ended William's schooling. His father got him a job as an apprentice to a Unitarian pawnbroker in Goose Gate, Nottingham's slums. Then within a year of his bankruptcy, William's father died, leaving a widow (who tried to eke out a living by selling toys, needles, and cotton), fourteen-year-old William (who had no take-home pay as an apprentice), and three young daughters, one of whom was an invalid.

In the next few years William saw as much of poverty as he ever wanted to see. His family was poor, but working as a pawnbroker, he saw many who were far poorer. He witnessed as poverty-stricken citizens battled soldiers and then broke into bakeries to get bread. He felt the injustice of high taxation and the inequity of the Corn Laws that protected the landowners at the expense of the poor. He even joined a political movement aimed at revolutionizing the British government.

But he also began attending a Methodist chapel in Nottingham. And one night, trudging home after a late meeting, he pondered all the deep thoughts that had been churning through his mind and decided to turn his life over to Jesus Christ. Undramatically, William Booth had become a Christian.

Six years later, having finished his appointed time as an apprentice, William tried to find a job, preferably at something unrelated to pawnbroking. But he was unsuccessful. After a year of unemployment in Nottingham, he decided to move to the big city of London. Those twelve months of unemployment were "among the most desolate of my life," William recalled later. "No one had the slightest interest in me."

London didn't seem much better than Goose Gate in Nottingham. If anything, the poverty was worse. Jobs were just as scarce. And the city, as William quickly discovered, literally stank. Smoke from three million chimneys blended in a putrid amalgam with gin, onions, dung, drying batter, and sewage. The River Thames had been appropriately nicknamed "The Great Stink."

Because he could find nothing else, he finally accepted work as a pawnbroker, a job that he was ashamed of for the rest of his life. His one joy in life came on Sundays when he often took the opportunity to preach, sometimes outdoors in a London park and sometimes in a small chapel eight miles away. It was a long walk.

He regretted he couldn't spend more time preaching, but that was impossible. "There is no way; no one wants me."

After all, the Methodists had just declined to renew his church membership (he had stubbornly refused to give up his open-air preaching in Kennington Common), and his application to serve as chaplain on a convict ship bound for Australia — a job hardly any self-respecting minister wanted — had been rejected. Besides that, a doctor had warned him that he was such a bundle of nervous energy that he probably wouldn't live too long. And now he was having increasing stomach problems and was rapidly developing ulcers.

So just as he was about to give up on everything, he met this businessman "angel" who wanted to enlist him as a minister with a group which had broken with the Methodists. Shortly thereafter, he met Catherine.

Catherine's mother was rigid, narrow, and sometimes neurotic. Her father was a backslidden

Methodist minister turned coachmaker, for whom both mother and daughter prayed. For a while he was active in the temperance movement, but eventually took to drink himself.

William Booth once said that Catherine's mother was "a woman of the sternest principle he had ever met.... To her, right was right no matter what it might entail." She refused to allow her daughter to study French because it might open the door to French novels and infidel literature. Most of Catherine's education was at home, because Mrs. Mumford was afraid of the companions with whom her daughter might have to mix at school. To avoid secular contamination, Catherine grew up without playmates. Instead she played church with her dolls and often preached to them. Table conversation was always adult and serious. The only other child in the family, a brother, left home as soon as he could (at age sixteen) to sail to America, and that left Catherine to be her mother's confidante.

Nervous and delicate, Catherine battled various health problems from childhood. When she was fourteen, curvature of the spine forced her to be bedridden for several months; when she was eighteen, tuberculosis forced her to leave home for the seashore town of Brighton for sixteen months. She returned to London from her convalescence about the time that William Booth came to London to hunt for a job.

It was said of Catherine: "Next to religion, she cared most for disputation." Strangely enough, that endeared her to William. He had never met anyone like her.

She had definite thoughts on almost everything, even as he had. She even had definite thoughts on the kind of man she wanted to marry. He would have to have religious views similar to hers; he would have to be a man of sense and character ("I could never respect a fool"); and he would have to have similar tastes. She also believed she must be physically attracted to him. Lastly, he must be a total abstainer. Besides that, she had a personal preference for a minister. William Booth met all the qualifications except for not being a total abstainer. She soon convinced him of the importance of total abstinence, and that made him her perfect match.

Within a month of their Good Friday tryst, Booth began having second thoughts about many things. People didn't seem to respond to his preaching; denominational officials were giving him the cold shoulder; congregations appeared to be so much better educated than he. Maybe he should return to pawnbroking so he and Catherine could get married. He shared his thoughts with Catherine.

In a "My dear friend" letter, she responded, "Never mind who frowns, if God smiles. The words, 'gloom, melancholy and despair,' lacerate my heart. Don't give way to such feelings for a moment. God loves you. He will sustain you. . . . The thought that I should increase your perplexity and cause you any suffering is almost unthinkable. I am tempted to wish that we have never seen each other. Do try to forget me."

William misunderstood the letter. He thought she was rejecting him, and dashed off a frantic note in response. She wrote back: "I fear you did not fully understand my difficulty. If you are satisfied that the step is not opposed to the will of God, let us be one, come what may." A few days later they were engaged.

The engagement came easily, compared to the marriage. Their wedding would have to wait for more than three years.

On the night of their engagement Catherine wrote: "The evening is beautifully serene and tranquil, according sweetly with the feelings of my soul. The whirlwind is past and the succeeding calm is in proportion to its violence. All is well. . . . The more you lead me up to Christ in all things, the more highly shall I esteem you; and if it be possible to love you more than I do now, the more I shall love you."

Because William traveled a great deal in the next three years, the correspondence of the engaged couple continued. His notes were short; hers were frequently twenty-five hundred to three thousand words in length. One biographer referred to them as "Puritan love letters." Perhaps, but there was also plenty of emotional warmth conveyed in them.

He spoke of his problems: "I walked eight miles yesterday. I ought to have ridden. I feel uncommonly tired and weary this morning. My head aches and I feel altogether out of order."

In her responses, she sometimes scolded him: "Don't sit up singing till twelve o'clock after a hard day's work. Such things are not required by either God or man, and remember you are not your own."

Sometimes she sounded schoolmarmish: "Try and cast off the fear of man," but soon she would sound human again: "You may justly consider me inadequate to advise you in spiritual matters, after living at so great a distance from God myself."

She knew that she shouldn't worry about him, but she did anyway. "The very fact of loving invests the being beloved with a thousand causes of care and anxiety, which, if unloved, would never exist. At least, I find it so."

Biographer William Nelson wrote, "It would never have done for a half-hearted man to have married Catherine Mumford." Some of her letters would have intimidated a lesser man. Once, she wrote, "I ought to restrain the tide of feeling more than I do in writing to you," but she said that she did not want to "cool or restrain it, so that you may know of what I am made."

She was not afraid to give him her pastoral advice: "I want you to be a man and a Christian and then I am satisfied.... I have such views of what the man must be to whom I give myself that it would be bitterer than gall to find myself bound to one in mind and head manifestly unworthy." Perhaps she was thinking of her parents' marriage, and a father who had lost interest in spiritual matters. "God is not glorified so much by preaching or teaching or anything else as by holy living."

Their marriage was delayed by financial reasons, but there were other problems as well. Booth couldn't find a congenial denomination. Before their engagement, both of them had left the Methodist Church (or were asked to leave) and had joined the Methodist Reformers. However, there was much bickering among the Reformers, and the lay leaders were vying with the clergy for power. So the young couple withdrew from the Reformers. Catherine began attending a Congregational Church and encouraged William to study for the Congregational ministry. But the books they gave him to read were too Calvinistic to fit his personal theology. William and Catherine didn't know where to turn until another small Methodist splinter group invited William to take a circuit of churches about one hundred miles north of London. Though it meant parting from Catherine, it was an opportunity he could not pass up.

One of his letters to Catherine describes his feelings: "I am still whirling about the country. Tonight I go back to Spalding; Tuesday to Rinchbeck; Wednesday to Suttleton; Thursday a special sermon at Boston. . . . I wish all this writing was at an end and that you were here, mine, in my arms, and yet I cannot help having fears and doubts about the future. How I wish the Reformers would amalgamate with the New Connexion or with the Association and that all this agitation were ended. . . . But I am always running before to find doubts and fears; mine has always been a restless and dissatisfied life, and I am fearful that it will continue so until I get safe to heaven."

In his restlessness he even thought of going to the United States and trying to become a Methodist preacher there. He asked Catherine if she was willing to go with him. She assured him that she was, but she cautioned him, in one of her more pastoral letters, against "ambition." "I see ambition to be your chief mental besetment. . . . Ambition even to save souls may not be sanctified. But ambition simply to glorify God, the soul risen up to the one sublime idea of glorifying God, must be sanctified."

While William was worrying, Catherine was preparing — preparing to be a minister's wife. "I enlarged the scope of my reading, wrote notes and made comments on all the sermons and lectures that appeared at all worthy of the trouble, started to learn shorthand. . . ."

The hardest thing for her to learn was the piano. William felt strongly that every minister's wife should play the piano, so she tried to learn. But it didn't come easily for Catherine. She lacked any musical sense. It was hard on her nerves; it made her irritable. She wrote: "Patience is a thing I am very deficient in. The music has tried me almost beyond endurance. I could freely abandon it and touch it no more. Once today I raised my eyes from the music and through some bitter tears looked at your likeness and said to myself, 'William, I do this for thee.' So I will persevere and I will for your sake go on. Measure my love for you by this standard."

What came easier for Catherine was writing sermons and outlines for her husband-to-be. He was so busy traveling from one of his circuit churches to another that he often dashed off notes to her such as "I want a sermon on the Flood, one on Jonah, and one on the Judgment. Send me some bare thoughts; some clear, startling outline. Nothing moves people like the terrific. They must have hell-fire flashed before their faces or they will not move."

Catherine obliged, although she occasionally reminded him to "watch against mere animal excitement in your revival services.... I never did like noise and confusion, only so far as I believed it to be the natural expression of deep anxiety wrought by the Holy Ghost; but my love, I do think noise made by the preacher and the Christians in the church is productive of evil only. I don't believe the Gospel needs such roaring and foaming to make it effective, and to some minds it would make it appear ridiculous, and bar them against its reception forever."

Catherine developed four rules for their future married life: (1) Never to have any secrets from my husband; (2) Never to have two purses; (3) Talk out differences of opinion to secure harmony and don't try to pretend the differences don't exist; (4) Never to argue in front of children.

The fact that two of the four had to do with differences of opinion underlines the fact that they were both opinionated people.

One area where they initially differed regarded women. He felt that a woman has more in the heart but a man has more in the head. Strongly disagreeing, she said that she would never marry a man who would not give to woman her proper due. She acknowledged that because of "inadequate education" most women were "inferior to man intellectually. . . . But that she is naturally so, I see no cause to believe."

William seemed to delight in the correspondence. Once he wrote: "I want you to hear me, to criticize me, to urge me on. I feel such a desperate sense of loneliness, so oppressive to my spirit. I speak and preach and act, and it is passed over; there is one with whom I can talk over my performance; to others I cannot mention it for fear of being thought egotistic or seeking for praise, and for some reasons others say little or nothing of it to me." Catherine never seemed reticent to speak out.

At times during the long engagement, Catherine seemed almost too willing to see the marriage postponed. Perhaps she enjoyed the intellectual intimacy more than she might the physical intimacy. But when he became discouraged, she talked radiantly about their future life together: "We will make home to each other the brightest spot on earth; we will be tender, thoughtful, loving and forbearing. . .yes, we will."

After a year on the Spalding Circuit, one hundred miles north of London, William joined another Methodist splinter group called the New Connexion and returned to London for six months of study. Catherine had encouraged him to make the move even though ministers had to wait four years before they were free to marry. William could hardly endure six months of schooling while thousands were dying and going to hell; and he didn't think much of the four years' probation before marriage either.

Fortunately, his tutor was lenient and allowed William to do more preaching than classroom study; also it was fortunate that the New Connexion made a special exception in William's case and agreed to let him get married after a probation of only one year.

Early in 1855, not quite twenty-six years old, William became an evangelist with the New Connexion. Once again as he was frequently separated from Catherine, he became depressed and lonely. He wrote her: "You know me; I am fitful, very; I mourn over it, I hate myself on account of it. But there it is; a dark column in the inner life of my spirit. You know it." Despite his depression, during four months of evangelistic efforts, he saw 1739 people profess decisions for Jesus Christ.

In June, William and Catherine, now both twenty-six, finally got married. It was a small and simple wedding with only her father, his sister, and the presiding minister present. After a one-week honeymoon, they left for his next evangelistic foray.

She wanted to accompany him everywhere — for his sake as well as hers — but her health couldn't take it. When Booth left her in London once, she wrote, "I feel as if part of myself were wanting."

A few months later she wrote her parents: "He is kinder and more tender than ever. Bless him! He is worth a bushel of the ordinary sort."

After eight months of an itinerating marriage, she wrote a letter to a friend, extolling her husband's preaching: "My precious William excelled himself and electrified the people. You would indeed have participated in my joy and pride could you have heard and seen what I did. Bless the Lord, O my soul."

The next paragraph was written with a bolder, less refined penmanship. "I have just come into the room where my dear little wife is writing this precious document and snatching the paper have read the above eulogistic sentiments. I just want to say that this very same night she gave me a curtain lecture on my blockheadism, stupidity, etc., and lo, she writes to you after this fashion. However, she is a precious, increasingly precious treasure to me, despite the occasional dressing down that I come in for."

Undaunted, Catherine resumed the letter in the next paragraph. "We have had a scuffle over the above, but I must let it go, for I have not time to write another, having an engagement at two o'clock, and it is now near one. But I must say in self-defense that it was not about the speech or anything important, that the said curtain lecture was given, but only on a point, which in no way invalidates the eulogy."

William loved his evangelistic work, but for one reason or another his fellow ministers in the New Connexion were not always as enthusiastic. So in 1858, after three extremely busy and successful years of evangelism, the Booths were assigned to a small ninety-member charge. But this small parish gave Catherine the opportunity to do some preaching herself.

When a nearby minister attacked women's right to preach, Catherine responded with a thirty-two page rebuttal. To her mother she wrote: "Would you believe that a congregation half composed of ladies could sit and hear such self-depreciatory rubbish?"

Despite the fact that William was "always pestering me to begin," Catherine had personally been timid to speak in public. But in 1860, after the birth of daughter Emma, she felt "divinely compelled" to say something in a church service. She said that she heard the devil telling her, "You will look like a fool." In reply, she said, "I have never yet been a fool for Christ. Now I will be one."

The personal word that she gave at the conclusion of the morning service was so well received that she was asked to speak in the evening. That began a speaking ministry in which she often was better received than her husband.

What made this remarkable, says author Richard Collier, was "Most Victorian women lived in a world of sandalwood fans, white kid-gloves and tortoise-shelled card cases; a respectable woman who raised her voice in public risked grave censure."

An article in The Gospel Guide described Catherine's style: "In dress nothing could be neater. A plain, black straw bonnet slightly relieved by a pair of dark violet strings; a black velvet loosely-fitting jacket, with tight sleeves, which appeared exceedingly suitable to her while preaching, and a black silk dress, constituted the plain and becoming attire of this female preacher. . . . Her delivery is calm, precise and clear without the least approach to formality or tediousness."

She never could understand why reports on sermons by women preachers seemed to concentrate more on fashion than on content.

Each year for four successive annual conferences, William waited for the New Connexion to reassign him back to evangelistic work. He felt he had been divinely called to evangelism and that the denomination was resisting the will of God. He couldn't understand why they didn't allow him to be an evangelist.

Catherine urged him to leave the denomination; William was cautious. He had a conservative streak. Catherine explained: "I do not see any honorable course for us but to resign at once, and risk all. But William is afraid. He thinks of me and the children; and I appreciate his loving care, but I tell him God will provide."

After the denomination's 1861 conference, the Booths left. With four young children and with no visible means of support, they stepped out in faith. To help with the finances, Catherine with almost too much willingness sold her piano. For the next four years, William, sometimes with Catherine by his side, conducted evangelistic missions up and down England.

Frequently Catherine had to stop to have a baby or to restore her health or to stabilize her young family; William had his ups and downs as well.

Once when Catherine was back in London he wrote her: "I have not been in very good spirits today. I have been looking at the dark side of myself. In fact, I can find no other side. I seem to be all dark, mentally, physically, spiritually. The Lord have mercy on me! I feel I am indeed so thoroughly unworthy of the notice of either God or man."

He was a man of moods. "On bad days, he grew tense and irritable," writes one biographer, "and his children learned to make themselves scarce. Only with Catherine did Booth all his life preserve the lover's tenderness."

His relationship with Catherine was unique and he knew it: "I am quite sure," he wrote her, "that we do now realize far more of this blissful union, this oneness, than very many around. I meet with but few who think and love and hate and admire and desire alike to the same extent that we do, and also with very few who realize as much domestic and conjugal felicity."

But after bearing six children in nine years, struggling with a wandering, homeless existence, facing recurrent health problems, and trying to cheer up William, Catherine became depressed herself. During this time she wrote, "I know I ought not to be depressed. I know it dishonors the Lord. But I cannot help it. I have struggled hard, more than anyone knows, for a long time against it. Sometimes I have literally held myself head and heart and hands, and waited for the floods to pass over me. Well, at present, I am under, under, under."

Her youngest baby was suffering from convulsions; she was having trouble paying the bills; she had her hands full with an active brood of children; and her spinal problems seemed to be returning. Meanwhile, William was caught up in the emotional excitement of successful revival meetings in northern England. So he wrote her: "Cheer up. All will be well. Whatever you do, don't be anxious."

He also advised her to seek some diversion. Not long afterwards, she received an invitation to conduct revival meetings herself, entirely apart from her husband, in south London. William encouraged her to accept the invitation and she did.

The meetings were so successful that they led to more invitations in other parts of London. Soon her husband came to London to join her.

She spoke to two to three hundred prostitutes at a meeting of the Midnight Movement for Fallen Women while William invaded the most neglected and underprivileged sections of the poverty-ridden city. Then came another turning point for the Booths.

"I remember it well," Catherine recalled. "William had come home one night tired out as usual. It was between eleven and twelve o'clock. Flinging himself into an easy chair, he said to me, 'Oh Kate, as I passed those gin palaces tonight I seemed to hear a voice saying, "Where can you go and find such heathen as these, and where is there so great a need for your labor?" '

"I remember," she added, "the emotion that this produced in my soul. This meant another start in life."

It also meant more financial problems. On the plus side it meant for Catherine a permanent home at last. And more importantly, it meant the launching of the East London Mission which gradually evolved into the Salvation Army.

The process wasn't easy.

As one author puts it, "This delicate and ill-educated man, married to a very sick woman, stood by himself on Mile End Waste and was pelted with garbage by the drunkards who reeled out of their gin palaces to deride and mock him."

William took his oldest son, Bramwell, into an East End pub and showed him the world of drunken women and violent men. Then he told his son, "These are our people. These are the people I want to live for and bring to Christ."

At home, however, William wasn't easy to live with. Perhaps he needed a place where he and Catherine could be alone without the children. His stomach problems caused him to be irritable and harsh-tempered. Undoubtedly he loved his children, but his love often came through more clearly from a distance. They got on his nerves. "His kisses," one writer says, "were more on paper than on their lips."

Biographer Begbie alleges that William was fond of his children, but was "too absorbed by his work, too distracted by anxieties, and too often tired by physical pain to give them the whole and perfect love of a father's heart."

He had a fetish for cleanliness and punctuality, and his children were whipped if they stepped out of line. Though he didn't take the title of the General of the Salvation Army until the late 1870s, he was already a general at home.

In 1868 Catherine gave birth to her eighth child, the last of the amazing brood of Booth children. In time all of them not only made their personal confessions of faith but also became active in the ministry. When he was sixteen, Bramwell was placed in charge of five Food-for-the-Million shops where the poor could buy food cheaply; by the time he was twenty, he was appointed as his father's Chief of Staff. Their second son, Ballington, was placed in charge of a training home for men when he was only twenty. Their oldest daughter, Katie, began preaching on the streets when she was only sixteen.

Once when she was asked the secret of raising a Christian family, Catherine responded: "The very first principle is that you acknowledge God's entire ownership of your children."

Each year the work increased. By 1870, there were a dozen preaching stations, besides evening classes, Ragged Schools, reading rooms, Penny Banks, Soup Kitchens, and Relief of the Destitute and Sick Poor, not to mention a new magazine (with occasional articles from Catherine as well as William) which eventually became known as the *War Cry*.

As the work grew, it took over their home. Even bedrooms doubled as offices. Catherine's only relief came when she was able to induce a friendly builder to put in a double ceiling packed with sawdust over a small sanctuary that she had. Later Catherine wrote: "From the attic to the kitchen every available scrap of space has been occupied with correspondence and secretaries.... The pressure upon the General and on my children was always so severe that, after putting in a good day's work, it seemed as if still more remained to be done, and so they would sit up over them til the small hours of the morning.... Only too glad would I have been if I could have retired to some little cottage corner where I could have buried myself in the privacy which, the more I loved, the less I seemed able to obtain."

Despite the rapid growth of the movement, the Booth family continued to flirt with bankruptcy. Somehow, Catherine, besides preaching and teaching and struggling with increasing health problems, had the reputation of being a good homemaker as well. In later years, their eldest son, Bramwell, described his mother this way: "She not only patched our clothes, but made us proud of the patches." A visitor who stopped in for tea was surprised to find Catherine darning her husband's socks.

Yet Catherine continued to be as strong-willed as ever. Sometimes she and William would dogmatically argue opposite points of view one night; then having been convinced by the other's arguments, each would switch and argue the opposite side the next evening. Early in their marriage, Catherine seemed to caution her husband against emotion in revival meetings; later in their married lives, they seem to have changed sides. Catherine's views on "holiness" teaching were always stronger than those of her husband, and from the start she opposed the administration of the sacraments (partly because she opposed giving wine to former alcoholics) while he took longer to make up his mind on the subject.

They also had an understandable disagreement when the brewers of London donated money to the Salvation Army. She wanted to send it back. His arguments prevailed. He argued that it was better to keep it and undo some of the mischief the brewers had done.

Financial pressures never let up. Earlier, she had been the optimist and he the pessimist; now the roles reversed. The continuing financial burdens weighed on her. "My precious husband is careworn and overwrought with this great work," she wrote in a letter. "The tug to get money — that is bad enough, but to have to think of self is worse than all.

"You will say, 'Where is your faith?' I fear it is very low. Yet I do hold on to the promises. I believe in some way the Lord will deliver us.... It seems very strange that the greatest abundance seems to go where they know least how to use it."

Then when William got gastric fever, a daughter got smallpox, and Catherine herself became ill again, depression returned: "My soul seems dumb before the Lord. A horror of great darkness comes over me at times. But, in the midst of it all, I believe He will do all things well."

It was in 1888 when the Booths were nearly sixty and the Salvation Army had become international with their children spreading the message into distant lands, that Catherine discovered a small cancerous growth on her breast. She was given about eighteen months to live.

She told her husband: "Do you know my first thought? My first thought was that I regretted that I should not be here to nurse you when you came to your last hour."

It was a crushing blow for William. He wrote in his diary: "I am sixty years old, and for the first time during all these long years, so far as memory serves me, has God in His infinite mercy allowed me to have any sorrow that I could not cast on Him." He could not understand it.

He spoke of one night when during "the great part of the night I had a strong conflict myself with the enemy, and great darkness and heaviness in my heart. . . . Life became a burden, almost too heavy to be borne."

Later he wrote: "To stand by the side of those you love and watch the ebbing tide of life, unable to stem it or to ease the anguish, while the stabs of pain make the eyes flash fire and every limb and nerve quivers, forcing cries of suffering from the courageous soul — is an experience of sorrow which words can but poorly describe."

During the months of her illness, she said she felt as if she were "dying in a railway station." It certainly seemed like it. Urgent telegrams came at all hours day and night. Lieutenants barged into the house reporting to General William or to Chief of Staff Bramwell. William or Bramwell was always leaving or returning on some Army business.

And Catherine herself was still deeply involved. For several months she continued preaching. When she became too weak to do more, the action came to her. Richard Collier writes in *The General Next to God*, "Her bedroom was the conference room where the finite points of the Army's expanding social policy were now argued and shaped."

Of course, William kept busy. As the months of her illness dragged by, he stayed closer to home. He was trying to keep his mind on writing a book, but it wasn't easy. Sometimes he would break down in tears, moaning, "How can it be? How can it be?"

But he continued to arise daily at six A.M. for a cold bath and two hours work before breakfast, which was often a boiled egg, buttered toast, and unsweetened hot tea.

It was amazing how rapidly the Salvation Army had grown. By 1890, there were 2,900 centers; about $50 million had been raised for the underprivileged; 10,000 Salvation Army officers were holding 50,000 meetings each week.

By this time, Catherine had a notable surgeon tending to her, Sir James Paget. She finally consented to surgery, but now it was too late. By 1890, Catherine had come to the end. She could no longer speak, so she pointed to a wall motto above the mantel, which said, "My grace is sufficient for thee."

After Catherine's death, the Army continued to flourish, but the close-knit Booth family started to unravel. Catherine was the one who had always held the strong-willed family members together. "I am your General first and your father afterwards," William told one daughter. Although they remained in Christian work and their zeal for God continued, six of the eight children eventually defected from the Salvation Army. With their defection, they also became estranged from their father.

One son who remained faithful to the Army and to William was Bramwell, his Chief of Staff. To him, William paid the highest compliment, "You are like her, Bramwell, your Mother."

When you put together two determined people like William and Catherine, both of whom came from problem marriages, you wouldn't expect to find the love and commitment that was evidenced by the Booths. They needed each other. At times they admonished one another; at other times, they propped each other up. The fact of the matter is, they loved each other.

It's an unusual army that is founded in love, but, of course, the Salvation Army has always been an unusual army.

BIBLIOGRAPHY

THE LUTHERS

Bainton, Roland. *Here I Stand.* Nashville: Abingdon Press, 1950.

D'Aubigne, J.H. Merle. *The Life and Times of Martin Luther.* Chicago: Moody Press, 1950.

Friedenthal, Richard. *Luther: His Life and Times.* New York: Harcourt, Brace, Jovanovitch Co., 1967.

Luther, Martin. *Table Talk.* New Canaan, CT: Keats Publishing Co., 1979.

Schwiebert, E.G. *Luther and His Times.* St. Louis: Concordia Publishing House, 1950.

THE WESLEYS

Ayling, Stanley. *John Wesley.* Cleveland: Collins-World, 1979.

Brailsford, Mabel. *A Tale of Two Brothers.* New York: Oxford University Press, 1954.

Flint, Charles. *Charles Wesley and His Colleagues.* Washington, D.C.: Public Affairs Press, 1957.

Lee, Umphrey. *The Lord's Horseman, John Wesley the Man.* Nashville: Abingdon Press, 1954.

Wesley, John. *The Heart of Wesley's Journal.* New Canaan, CT: Keats Publishing Co., 1979.

THE EDWARDS

Dodds, Elisabeth D. *Marriage to a Difficult Man*. Philadelphia: Westminster Press, 1971.

Hitt, Russell T., ed. *Heroic Colonial Christians*. Philadelphia: J.B. Lippincott Co., 1966.

Miller, Perry. *Jonathan Edwards*. Westport, CT: Greenwood Publishers, 1949.

Winslow, Ola Elizabeth. *Jonathan Edwards*. New York: Macmillan Publishing Co., 1947.

Wood, James Playstead. *Mr. Jonathan Edwards*. New York: Seabury Press, 1968.

Wright, Elliott. *Holy Company*. New York: Macmillan Publishing Co., 1980.

THE MOODYS

Bradford, Gamaliel. *D.L. Moody, A Worker in Souls*. Doran and Company, 1927.

Curtis, Richard K. *They Called Him Mr. Moody*. Garden City, NY: Doubleday & Co., Inc., 1962.

Findlay, James J., Jr. *D.L. Moody, American Evangelist*. Chicago: University of Chicago Press, 1969.

Moody, Paul D. *My Father*. Boston: Little, Brown & Co., 1938.

Moody, William R. *The Life of D.L. Moody*. Old Tappan, NJ: Fleming H. Revell Co., 1900.

Pollock, J.C. *Moody*. New York: Macmillan Publishing Co., 1963.

THE BOOTHS

Beardsley, Frank G. *Heralds of Salvation*. New York: American Tract Society, 1939.

Begbie, Harold. *The Life of General William Booth*. New York: Macmillan Publishing Co., 1920.

Booth-Tucker, F.deL. *The Life of Catherine Booth*. Old Tappan, NJ: Fleming H. Revell Co., 1892.

Collier, Richard. *The General Next to God*. Cleveland: Collins-World, 1976.

Nelson, William. *General William Booth*. New York: Doran and Company, 1929.